AF417738

Pramesh Universal India
All Rights Reserved

© Publisher

All rights are reserved. No Part of this book may be reproduced, stored in a retrival system or transmitted in any form or by any means, electronic, mechanical, photocopying, recording or otherwise, without prior permission of the publisher.
All disputes subject to Bhopal (MP) jurisdiction only.

Title: Trading vocabulary
Edition: First Edition

Corporate Office:
85, Sudama Sun City, Piplani, BHEL, Bhopal, MP, India 462022

ISBN 13: 978-93-92363-10-8
ISBN 10: 93-92363-10-9

For any further information, write us at <u>prameshelib@gmail.com</u>

A to Z

☑ **Account closure (depositor account)**

The closure of beneficiary and pool accounts by the investor and the clearing member or at the discretion of the participant, if the client has defaulted in its obligations towards the participant.

☑ **Accounts Payable**

A current liability showing the amounts due to others within a period of one year when such liability resulted from the purchase or manufacturing of inventory.

☑ **Accounts Receivable**

Any money due to a business for merchandise or securities that it has sold or for services it has rendered. This is a key determinant in analyzing a company's liquidity.

☑ **Accreting**

A description applicable to a range of instruments, e.g. caps, swaps, collars and swaptions, where the notional amount on which the instrument is based increases successively during its life.

☑ **Accrued Interest**

The interest accruing on a security since the previous coupon date. If a security is sold between two payment dates, the buyer usually compensates the seller for the interest accrued, either within the price or as a separate payment.

☑ **Acid Test Ratio**

The value of cash equivalents and accounts receivable (the quick assets) divided by current liabilities. Also known as quick asset ratio or liquidity ratio, it is a measurement of corporate liquidity.

☑ **Acquirer**

Any individual/company/any other legal entity, which intends to acquire or acquires substantial quantity of shares or voting rights of target company or acquires or agrees to acquire control over the target company along with the persons acting in concert.

☑ **Active portfolio Strategy**

A strategy that uses available information and forecasting techniques to seek a better performance than a portfolio that is simply diversified broadly.

☑ **Adhoc Margin**

Margin collected by the Stock Exchange from the members having unduly large outstanding position or the margin levied on volatile scrips based on adhoc basis keeping in view the risk perspective.

☑ **Adjustable Peg**

Term for an exchange rate regime where a country's exchange rate is pegged (i.e. fixed) in relation to another currency (normally the dollar), but where the rate may be changed from time to time.

☑ **Adjusted beta**

The estimation of a security's future beta, which is derived from historical date, but is modified assuming that the security's real beta has tendency to move towards the market average of one.

☑ Admission to Dealing

The process of granting permission to the securities of a company to be listed in a Stock Exchange and to provide trading facilities for the securities in the market.

☑ Advance/Decline line

A technical analysis tool representing the total of differences between advances and declines of security prices. The advance/decline line is considered the best indicator of market movement as a whole.

Stock indices such as Dow-Jones Industrial Average only tell us the strength of 30 stocks where as the Advance/Decline line provides much more insight.

☑ Adviser

A financial planner or financial intermediary who offers advice on personal financial matters. Advisers may be paid an upfront or an ongoing commission for the investments that they recommend.

☑ Agency Orders

Orders that a broker dealer executes for the account of a customer with another professional or retail investor.

☑ Allotment Advice

A letter sent to the successful applicant by the company stating allotment of shares or debentures or other securities against his application. The advice is not negotiable in the market.

☑ **Allotment Letter**

Document of title issued to investors by companies stating allotment of shares/debentures /other securities to applicants subscribing for such securities or in pursuance of certain contracts entered into in that behalf. These letters are negotiable in the market.

☑ **Alpha**

In a Jensen Index, a factor to represent the portfolio's performance that diverges from its beta, representing a measure of the manager's performance.

☑ **AMBI**

Association of Merchant Bankers in India

☑ **American Depository Receipts (ADR) (U.S.)**

A certificate issued in the United States in lieu of a foreign security. The original securities are lodged in Bank/Custodian abroad, and the American Depository Receipts (ADRs) are traded in the US for all intents and purposes as if they were a domestic stock. An ADR dividend is paid in US dollars, so it provides a way for American investors to buy foreign securities without having to go abroad, and without having to switch in and out of foreign currencies.

☑ **American Option**

A put or call that can be exercised at any time prior to expiration. Most listed stock options, including those on European exchanges are US style options. Important exceptions are certain low strike price. options and options on shares with restricted transferability. Most listed options on other instruments are also US-style options, but a number of European style options have been introduced in recent years, particularly on stock indices and currencies.

☑ **AMFI**

Association of Mutual Funds in India

☑ **Analyst**

A firm / company / an individual who is engaged either on his own behalf or on behalf of any other firm or organization that is regularly publishing securities recommendations based on research either through print media and /or electronic media.

☑ **Appreciation**

A rise in the price of a security or in the value of one currency in terms of another.

☑ **Approved intermediary**

A person duly registered by the SEBI Board under the Securities Lending Scheme , 1997 through whom the lender of securities will deposit the securities and the borrower will borrow the securities.

☑ **Arbitrage**

1) Technically, arbitrage consists of purchasing a commodity or security in one market for immediate sale in another market (deterministic arbitrage).

2) Popular usage has expanded the meaning of the term to include any activity which attempts to buy a relatively underpriced item and sell a similar, relatively overpriced item, expecting to profit when the prices resume a more appropriate theoretical or historical relationship (statistical arbitrage).

3) In trading options, convertible securities, and futures, arbitrage techniques can be applied whenever a strategy involves buying and selling packages of related instruments.

4) Risk arbitrage applies the principles of risk offset to mergers and other major corporate developments. The risk offsetting position(s) do not insulate the investor from certain event risks (such as termination of a merger agreement on the risk of completion of a transaction within a certain time) so that the arbitrage is incomplete.

5) Tax arbitrage transactions are undertaken to share the benefit of differential tax rates or circumstances of two or more parties to a transaction.

6) Regulatory arbitrage transactions are designed to provide indirect access to a risk management market where one party is denied direct access by law or regulation.

7) Swap driven arbitrage transactions are motivated by the comparative advantages which swap counter-parties enjoy in different debt and currency markets. One counterparty may borrow at a relatively lower rate in the intermediate or long term United States dollar market, while the other

may have a comparative advantage in floating rate sterling.

For example: if stock is trading out $20 from one Market and $21 on other markets, the trader must buy shares at $20 from one Market and sell them for $21 on the different Market, getting the difference amount between both the markets price.

☑ **Arbitration**

An alternative dispute resolution mechanism provided by a stock exchange for resolving disputes between the trading members and their clients in respect of trades done on the exchange

☑ **Asian option**

An option whose pay-off depends on the average value of an underlier over a specified period.

☑ **Ask Price**

Ask price is a specific price at which you are looking to sell a share.

☑ **Asset Allocation**

The process of determining the optimal division of an investor's portfolio among different assets. Most frequently this refers to allocations between debt, equity, and cash

☑ **Asset allocation fund**

A mutual fund that splits its investment assets among stocks, bonds, and other vehicles in an attempt to provide a consistent return for the investor.

☑ Asset-backed securities

Securities backed by assets that are not mortgage loans. Examples include assets backed by automobile loans, credit card receivables and others.

☑ Asset based securitization

A process that creates a series of securities which is collaterised by assets mortgaged against loans, assets leased out, trade receivables, or assets sold on hire purchase basis or installment contracts on personal property.

☑ Asset Management

The function of managing assets on behalf of a customer, usually for a fee.

Asset Management Company The company which handles the day to day operations and investment decisions of a unit trust.

☑ Asset Stripper

A person who buys a company in order to make profit by peeling off its assets bit by bit, and then selling them. These assets may be separate subsidiaries or plant and equipment or property. This process invariably involves the stripping of another sort of asset (the employees) of a number of jobs. This has been largely responsible for giving asset strippers a bad name. The asset stripper relies on there being a difference in the price of the business as a whole (as valued by a stock market, for example) and the sum of the amounts that can be raised from its parts sold separately. Such a possibility arises most commonly when a company is making losses or a much smaller profit than seems to be justified by its size

☑ Asymmetric information

A situation where access to information by one party (or parties) to a transaction is better than access by another party (or parties). Asymmetric information can be used as a source of power in determining the outcome of the transaction.

☑ At Best

An instruction from the client to the broker authorizing him to use his discretion so as to execute an order at the best possible market price.

☑ At-the-Money Option

Term used to describe an option or a warrant with an exercise price equal to the current market price of the underlying asset

☑ Auction

When a seller is not in a position to deliver the securities he has sold, the buyer sends in his applications for buying-in, so that the securities can be bought from the market and delivered to him. This process by which the securities are procured on behalf of the defaulter is known as Auction.

☑ **Auditor**

A person who is professionally qualified to examine and scrutinize accounts. He/she inspects records and reports on the profitability and financial position of the company.

☑ **Aunt Jane/Aunt Agatha**

A passive long term investor.

☑ **Authorized Assistants**

Assistants or clerks of members who are authorized by them to do business on their behalf in the market. The member has to take responsibility of fulfilling all the transactions and business commitments of the authorized assistants entered into on behalf of the members.

☑ **Authorized Capital**

The amount of capital that a company has been authorized to raise by way of equity and preference shares, as mentioned in the Articles of Association / Memorandum of Association of the company.

☑ **Automatic Reinvestment**

A fund service giving unit holders/ shareholders the option to purchase additional units/ shares using dividend and capital gain distributions.

☑ **Average Annual Growth Rate – AAGR**

The average increase in the value of a portfolio over the period of a year .

☑ Annual Report

An annual report is a yearly report that every company prepares to impress the shareholders of their company. The annual report consists of lots of information about a company, from cash flow to management strategy.

Several people read the annual report to look at the company's solvency and judge their financial position

☑ Averaging

The process of gradually buying more and more securities in a declining market (or selling in a rising market) in order to level out the purchase (or sale) price.

☑ Averaging Down

Averaging down means the investor buys more stock when the price of a particular stock goes down. This decreases the average purchase price of your specific stock. Several investors use this strategy if they feel that consensus about a specific company is wrong, so they expect the stock price to jump back and earn profit.

☑ Baby Bond (U.S)

A bond with a face value of less than $1000 usually in $100 denominations.

☑ Back office

The part of a firm that is responsible for post-trade activities. Depending upon the organisational structure of the firm, the back office can be a single department or multiple units (such as documentation, risk management, accounting or settlements). Some firms have combined a portion of these responsibilities, usually found in the back office, particularly those related to risk management, into what they term as a middle office function.

☑ **Backwardation/Ulta Badla/Undha Badla**

The payment of money charges made by a seller of shares which he borrows to deliver against his sale. These charges become payable only when there are more sellers who are not in a position to deliver against their sale. These charges become payable to the buyer, when the seller is not in a position to deliver the documents to the buyers who demand delivery.

☑ **Badla**

Carrying forward of transactions from one settlement period to another without effective delivery. This is permitted only in specified securities and is done at the making up price which is usually the closing price of the last day of settlement.

☑ **Badla Charge/ Contango**

Consideration or interest paid to the seller by the buyer for carrying over a transaction from one settlement period to another.

☑ **Badliwalas**

A financier who lends money to both buyers and sellers of shares when they are not able to pay or deliver.

☑ Bail out of issue

When the public issue do not get good response from the public or fails to garner minimum subscription, the issuer or promoters approaches the financiers or some persons to arrange subscription to bail out the issue for consideration of buy-back shares subsequent from the financiers at higher price or compensating the financier by payment of interest on the amount of the subscription money paid in the public issue.

☑ Balance Sheet

An accounting statement of a company's assets and liabilities, provided for the benefit of shareholders and regulators. It gives a snapshot, at a specific point of time, of the assets that the company holds and how the assets have been financed.

☑ Balanced fund

Funds which aim to provide both growth and regular income as such schemes invest both in equities and fixed income securities in the proportion indicated in their offer documents.

☑ Bancassurance

The phenomenon whereby a financial institution combines the selling of banking products and insurance products through the same distribution channel. Popular in the early 1990s bancassurance rested on the premise that it is easy to cross-sell banking and insurance services because customers feel confident buying insurance from the same institution where they keep their savings.

☑ **Band Ke Bhao**

Unauthorized trading in securities done outside official hours.

☑ **Bankers acceptance**

A short-term credit investment created by a non-financial firm and guaranteed by a bank to make payment. Acceptances are traded at discounts from face value in the secondary market

☑ **Bank investment contract**

A security with an interest rate guaranteed by a bank. It provides a specific yield on a portfolio over a specified period.

☑ **Banker to an issue**

A scheduled bank carrying on all or any of the issue related activities namely acceptance of application and application monies; acceptance of allotment or call monies; refund of application monies; and payment of dividend or interest warrants.

☑ **Basis**

In a futures market, basis is defined as the cash price (or spot price) of whatever is being traded minus its futures price for the contract in question. It is important because changes in the relationship between cash and futures prices affect the values of using futures as a hedge. A hedge, however, will always reduce risk as long as the volatility of the basis is less than the volatility of the price of whatever is being hedged.

☑ **Basis Point**

One hundredth of a percentage point. Basis points are used in currency and bond markets where the size of trades mean that large amounts of money can change hands on small price movements . Thus if the yield on a Treasury bill rose from 5.25% to 5.33% the change would have been eight basis points.

☑ **Basis Risk**

The risk that the relationship between the prices of a security and the instrument used to hedge it will change, thereby reducing the effectiveness of the hedge. In other words ,risk of varying fluctuations of the spot and the futures price between the moment at which a position is opened and the moment at which it is closed.

☑ **Basis of Allotment**

An allotment pattern of an issue among different categories of applicant

☑ **Bear**

A pessimist market operator who expects the market price of shares to decline. The term also refers to the one who has sold shares which he does not possess, in the hope of buying them back at a lower price, when the market price of the shares come down in the near future.

☑ **Bear Hug**

A variety of takeover strategy that seeks to hurry target company managements to recommend acceptance of a tender offer in a short period of time.

☑ **Bear Market**

It is a market where investors talk about the stock market performing in a downward trend, or it is a certain period where the prices of multiple stocks are falling.

☑ **Bear Trap**

A false signal indicating that the rising trend of a stock or index has reversed when in fact it has not. This can occur during a bear market reversal when short sellers believe the markets will sink back to its declining ways. If the market continues to rise, the shorters get trapped and are forced to cover their position at higher prices.

☑ **Bearer Securities/Bearer Bonds**

Securities which do not require registration of the name of the owner in the books of the company. Both the interest and the principal whenever they become due are paid to anyone who has possession of the securities. No endorsement is required for changing the ownership of such securities.

☑ **Behavioral economics**

Combination of psychology and economics that investigates what happens in markets in which some of the agents display human limitations and complications (i.e. irrational behavior).

☑ **Bellweather**

A security that is seen as a significant indicator of the direction in which a market's price is moving.

☑ **Bench Mark**

Security used as the basis for interest rate calculations and for pricing other securities. Also denotes the most heavily traded and liquid security of a particular class

☑ **Benchmark index**

Indicators used to provide a point of reference for evaluating a fund's performance

☑ **Beneficial owner**

The true owner of a security. Registered holder of the shares may act as a nominee to the true shareholders/owners.

☑ **Benefit cost ratio**

A ratio attempting to clearly identify the relationship between the cost and benefits of a proposed project. This ratio is used to measure both quantitative and qualitative projects, as sometimes benefits and costs cannot be measured exclusively on financial terms.

☑ **Beta**

A measure of the volatility of a stock relative to the market index in which the stock is included. A low beta indicates relatively low risk; a high beta indicates a high risk.

☑ **Bid**

An offer of a price to buy as in an auction. Business on the Stock Exchange is done through bids. Bid also refers to the price one is willing to pay for a security.

☑ **Bid Spread**

The difference between the stated and /or displayed price at which a market maker is willing to sell a security and the price at which he is willing to buy it.

☑ **Bid – Ask spread**

The difference between the bid price and the ask price.

☑ **Bid Price**

A bid price is nothing but the amount that you desire to pay for a particular share.

☑ **Bilateral netting**

An arrangement between two parties in which they exchange only the net difference in their obligations to each other. The primary purpose of netting is to reduce exposure to credit/settlement risk.

☑ **Black-Scholes model**

A mathematical model that provides a valuation technique for options. The model was adapted to provide a framework for valuing options in futures contracts.

☑ **Blank Transfer**

Where the name of the transferee is left blank on share transfer form, it constitutes a blank transfer. A person depositing shares with a stock broker for immediate or eventual sale, has to sign a blank transfer form. It is also done when shares are mortgaged, so that in the event of non payment the mortgager can fill in his own name in the transferee column and sell the share.

☑ **Block Trading**

Buying and selling a block of securities usually takes place when restructuring or liquidating a large portfolio.

☑ **Blow Out**

A security offering that sells out almost immediately.

☑ **Blue Chip**

The best rated shares with the highest status as investment based on return, yield, safety, marketability and liquidity.

☑ **Blue Sky Laws (U.S)**

Laws passed by the states in the U.S. to protect investors. The term traces its origin to a remark made by a Kansas legislator that unless a state passed effective legislation promoters would try to sell shares in the blue sky to unsuspecting investors.

☑ **Boiler Room (U.S)**

It is a practice of using high pressure sales tactics.This practice is sometimes used by stock brokers who try to sell investors the firm's house stock. A broker using boiler room tactics only gives customers promising information about the company and discourages them from doing any outside research.

☑ **Bond**

A negotiable certificate evidencing indebtedness- a debt security or IOU, issued by a company, municipality or government agency. A bond investor lends money to the issuer and, in exchange, the issuer promises to repay the loan amount on a specified maturity date. The issuer usually pays the bondholder periodic interest payments over the life of the loan.

☑ **Bond Trust**

Public unit trust which invests in government fixed interest or corporate fixed interest securities and investments.

☑ **Bonus Shares**

Shares issued by companies to their shareholders free of cost by capitalization of accumulated reserves from the profits earned in the earlier years.

☑ **Book building process**

A process undertaken by which a demand for the securities proposed to be issued by a corporate body is elicited and built up and the price for such securities is assessed for the determination of the quantum of such securities to be issued by means of a notice, circular, advertisement, document or information memoranda or offer document

☑ **Book Closure**

The periodic closure of the Register of Members and Transfer Books of the company, to take a record of the shareholders to determine their entitlement to dividends or to bonus or right shares or any other rights pertaining to shares.

☑ **Book Runner**

A Lead Merchant Banker who has been appointed by the issuer company for maintaining the book. The name of the Book Running Lead Manager will be mentioned in the offer document of the Issuer Company.

☑ **Book Value**

The net amount shown in the books or in the accounts for any asset, liability or owners' equity item. In the case of a fixed asset, it is equal to the cost or revalued amount of the asset less accumulated depreciation. Also called carrying value. The book value of a firm is its total net assets, i.e. the excess of total assets over total liabilities

☑ **Boom**

A condition of the market denoting increased activity with rising prices and higher volume of business resulting from greater demand of securities. It is a state where enlarged business, both investment and speculative, has been taking place for a sufficiently reasonable period of time.

☑ **Breadth of the Market**

The number of securities listed on the market in which there is regular trading.

☑ **Break**

A rapid and sharp decline in a security or index.

☑ **Break Even Point**

The stock price (or price) at which a particular strategy of transaction neither makes nor loses money. In options, the result is at the expiration date in the strategy. A dynamic break-even point changes as time passes.

☑ **Broad based Fund (sub account)**

A fund which has at least 20 shareholders and no single investor holds more than 10% of shares and units of the Fund. In case, if any investor holds more than 10% of shares or units of the fund, then it should be broad based.

☑ **Broker**

A member of a Stock Exchange who acts as an agent for clients and buys and sells shares on their behalf in the market. Though strictly a stock broker is an agent, yet for the performance of his part of the contract both in the market and with the client, he is deemed as a principal, a peculiar position of dual responsibility.

☑ Brokerage

Commission payable to the stockbroker for arranging sale or purchase of securities. Scale of brokerage is officially fixed by the Stock Exchange. Brokerage scales fixed in India are the maximum chargeable commission.

☑ Broker dealer

Any person, other than a bank engaged in the business of buying or selling securities on its own behalf or for others.

☑ BSE

The Bombay Stock Exchange (BSE) is the oldest stock exchange in India and Asia. It was established in 1875 under a banyan tree by five stockbrokers. Currently 5,400 shares are listed on BSE.

☑ Bubble

A speculative sharp rise in share prices which like the bubble is expected to suddenly burst.

☑ Bucket Shop (U.S)

A fraudulent brokerage firm that uses aggressive telephone sales tactics to sell securities that the brokerage owns and wants to get rid of. The securities that they sell are typically poor investment opportunities, almost always penny stocks.

A brokerage that makes trades on a client's behalf and promises a certain price. The brokerage, however, waits until a different price arises and then makes the trade, keeping the difference as profit.

A stock brokerage operation in which the broker accepts the client's money without ever buying the stock ordered. Instead the money is used for another purpose, the broker gambling that the customer is wrong and that the market price will decline and the stock can be bought at a lower price.

☑ **Bucketing**

A situation where, in an attempt to make a short-term profit, a broker confirms an order to a client without actually executing it. If the eventual price that the order is executed at is higher than the price available when the order was submitted, the customer simply pays the higher price. On the other hand, if the execution price is lower than the price available when the order was submitted, the customer pays the higher price and the brokerage firm pockets the difference. It also means directly or indirectly taking the opposite side of client's order into the brokers own account or into an account in which the broker has interest, without open and competitive execution of the order on an exchange.

☑ **Bull**

A market player who believes prices will rise and would, therefore, purchase a financial instrument with a view to selling it at a higher price. Opposite of a bear.

☑ **Bull Market**

It is a market where investors talk about the stock market performing in an upward trend, or it is a certain period where the prices of multiple stocks are increasing.

☑ **Bulldog Bond**

A bond denominated in sterling but issued by a non British borrower.

☑ **Buoyancy**

A rising trend in prices.

☑ **Business Day**

A day on which the Stock Exchange is open for business and trading in securities.

☑ **Butterfly spread**

An option strategy involving the simultaneous sale of an at the money straddle and purchase of an out of the money strangle. Potential gains will be seen if the underlying remains stable while the risk is limited should the underlying move dramatically. It's also the simultaneous buying and selling of call options at different exercise prices or at different expiry dates.

☑ **Buy back**

The repurchase by a company of its own stock or bonds

☑ **Buyer's Comparison Memo/Objection Statement**

Since normally comparison memos are only issued to the seller, the buyer figuring in the memo may not have any idea about the rejection by the computer of that transaction till the seller contacts him. Therefore, he is issued a Buyers Comparison Memo.

☑ **Buying - In**

When a seller fails to deliver shares to a buyer on the stipulated date, the buyer can enforce delivery by buying - in against the seller in an auction.

☑ **Buy on margin**

To buy shares with money borrowed from the stockbroker, who maintains a margin account for the customer.

☑ **CEDEL**

One of the two major organizations in the Eurobond market which clears or handles the physical exchange of, securities and stores securities. Based in Luxembourg, the company is owned by several shareholding banks and operates through a network of agents.

☑ **Calendar spread**

The simultaneous sale and purchase of either calls or puts with the same strike price but different expiration months.

☑ **Call Money**

The unpaid installment of the share capital of a company, which a shareholder is called upon to pay.

☑ **Call option**

An agreement that gives an investor the right, but not the obligation, to buy an instrument at a known price by a specified date. For this privilege, the investor pays a premium, usually a fraction of the price of the underlying security.

☑ **Capital Asset Pricing Model (CAPM)**

An economic theory that describes the relationship between risk and expected return and serves as a model for the pricing of risky securities. The CAPM asserts that the only risk that is priced by rational investors is systematic risk, because it cannot be eliminated by diversification. The CAPM says that the expected return of a security or a portfolio is equal to the rate on a risk-free security plus a risk premium.

☑ **Capital Gain Distribution**

Profits distributed to unit holders / shareholders resulting from the sale of securities held in the fund's portfolio for more than one year.

☑ **Carry Over Margin**

The margin fixed by the Stock Exchange and payable by the members for carrying over the transactions from one settlement period to another.

☑ **Cash List**

List of non-specified securities, traded usually for hand delivery and also for special delivery and spot delivery.

☑ **Cash Market**

A market for sale of security against immediate delivery, as opposed to the futures market.

☑ **Cash Settlement**

The settlement provision on some options and futures contracts that do not require delivery of the underlying security. For options, the difference between the settlement price on the underlying asset and the option's exercise price is paid to the option holder at exercise. For futures contracts, the exchange establishes a settlement price on the final day of trading and all remaining open positions are marked to market at that price.

☑ **Cats and Dogs (U.S)**

Stocks in companies that are small, new, poorly financed or in trouble.

CDSC (Contingent deferred sales charge)

A type of back end load sales charge, a contingent deferred sales charge is a fee charged when shares are redeemed within a specific period following their purchase. These charges are usually assessed on a sliding scale, with the fee reduced each year during which the shares are held.

☑ Central Listing Authority

The authority set up to address the issue of multiple listing of the same security and to bring about uniformity in the due diligence exercise in scrutinising all listing applications on any stock exchanges. The functions include processing the application made by any body corporate, Mutual Fund or collective investment scheme for the letter of recommendation to get listed at the stock exchange, making recommendations as to listing conditions and any other functions as may be specified by SEBI Board from time to time.

☑ Certificate of Deposit

A negotiable certificate issued by a bank, usually for a period of one month to a year, as evidence of an interest bearing time deposit. This may also be offered at a discount.

☑ Chalu Upla

Adjustment of position between two brokers either to avoid margin or to cross the trading or exposure limit.

☑ Chartist analysis

Using charts of financial asset price movements (often with the aid of additional descriptive statistics) to try to infer the likely course of future prices and thus construct forecasts and trading strategies.

☑ Cheapest to Deliver Issue

The acceptable Treasury security with the highest implied repo rate. It is the rate that a seller of a futures contract can earn by buying an issue and then delivering it at the settlement date.

☑ Chinese walls

Artificial barriers to the flow of information set up in large firms to prevent the movement of sensitive information between departments.

☑ Churning

An unethical practice employed by some brokers to increase their commissions by excessively trading in a client's account. In the context of the stock market, churning refers to a period of heavy trading with few sustained price trends and little movement in stock market indices.

☑ Circuit Breaker

A system to curb excessive speculation in the stock market, applied by the Stock Exchange authorities, when the index spurts or plunges by more than a specified per cent. Trading is then suspended for some time to let the market cool down.

☑ Circular trading

A fraudulent trading scheme where sell or buy orders are entered by a person who knows that the same number of shares at the same time and for the same price either have been or will be entered. These trades do not represent a real change in the beneficial ownership of the security. These trades are entered with the intention of raising or depressing the prices of securities.

☑ **Clean Float**

Where there is no official intervention – the price is permitted to vary in line with the market forces

☑ **Clearing**

Settlement or clearance of accounts, for a fixed period in a Stock Exchange.

☑ **Clearing House**

A department of an exchange or a separate legal entity that provides a range of services related to the clearance and settlement of trades and the management of risks associated with the resulting contracts. A clearing house is often central counterparty to all trades, that is, the buyer to every seller and the seller to every buyer.

☑ **Clearing member**

A member of a clearing corporation or clearing house of the derivatives exchange or derivatives segment of an exchange, who may clear and settle transactions in securities.

☑ Close-out-netting

An arrangement to settle all contracted but not yet due obligations to and claims on a counterparty by one single payment, immediately upon the occurrence of one of the defined events of default.

☑ Closing Out

Where a party to a contract does not make delivery against sale or payment against delivery of documents, the other party can close out the transaction against the defaulting party. The gain or loss arising from the closing out is borne by the defaulter.

☑ Close-ended Fund

A type of investment company that has a fixed number of shares which are publicly traded. The price of a closed end share fluctuates based on investor supply and demand. Closed ended funds are not required to redeem shares and have managed portfolios.

☑ Closing Price

The rate at which the last transaction in a security is struck before the close of the trading hours.

☑ Coercive Tender Offer

A tender offer that exerts pressure on target shareholders to tender early. This pressure may come in the form of preferential compensation for early tendering shareholders. Changes in securities laws have limited the effectiveness of such tender offers.

☑ Collar Agreement

Agreed upon adjustments in the number of shares offered in a stock-for-stock exchange to account for fluctuations in stock prices prior to the completion of the deal.

☑ Collateralised Mortgage Obligation (CMO)

A generic term for a security backed by real estate mortgages. CMO payment obligations are covered by interest and /or principal payments from a pool of mortgages. In addition to its generic meaning, CMO usually suggest a non governmental issue.

☑ Collective Investment Management Company

A company incorporated under the provisions of the Companies Act, 1956 and registered with SEBI under the SEBI (Collective Investment Schemes) Regulations, 1999, whose object is to organise,

operate and manage a Collective Investment Scheme.

☑ Collective investment scheme (CIS)

Any scheme or arrangement made or offered by any company under which the contributions, or payments made by the investors, are pooled and utilized with a view to receive profits, income, produce or property, and is managed on behalf of the investors is a Collective Investment Scheme. Investors do not have day to day control over the management and operation of such scheme or arrangement.

☑ **Commercial Paper**

A short term promise to repay a fixed amount that is placed on the market either directly or through a specialized intermediary. It is usually issued by companies with a high credit standing in form of a promissory note redeemable at par to the holder on maturity and therefore does not require any guarantee.

☑ **Common stock**

Units of ownership of a public corporation. Holders of common stock typically have voting rights and receive dividends, but there is no guarantee of dividend payment.

☑ **Competitive Bid**

An offer made by a person other than the acquirer who has made the first public announcement.

☑ **Composite issues**

An issue of securities by a listed company on a public-cum rights basis offered through a single offer document wherein the allotment for both public and rights component of the issue is proposed to be made simultaneously.

☑ **Compulsory delisting**

Permanent removal of securities of a listed company from a stock exchange as a penalizing measure at the behest of the stock exchange for not making submissions / complying with various requirements set out in the Listing agreement within the time frames prescribed.

☑ **Confirmation process**

The procedure for verifying trade details with a counterparty. This is generally done by exchanging via fax or mail a document (i.e. a confirmation) identifying the trade details and any governing legal documentation and verifying the accuracy of the information provided by the counterparty (i.e. matching).

☑ **Constituent Subsidiary General Ledger (SGL) account**

A constituent SGL account is an account held by an intermediary at Reserve Bank of India (RBI) on behalf of its constituents who have empowered the said intermediary to carry out various transactions on their behalf. In this account only constituent transactions can take place and under no circumstances the intermediary will use this account for proprietary transactions.

☑ **Continuous disclosure**

Procedure where certain companies are required to make disclosures on a continuing basis of their business activities by filing documents.

☑ **Continuous net settlement**

Automated book-entry accounting system that centralizes the settlement of compared security transactions and maintains an orderly flow of security and money balances.

☑ Contract Month

The month in which futures contracts may be settled by making or accepting delivery.

☑ Contract Note

A note issued by a broker to his constituent setting out the number of securities bought or sold in the market along with the rate, time and date of contract.

☑ Control of management

The right to appoint directly or indirectly or by virtue of agreements or in any other manner majority of directors on the Board of the target company or to control management or policy decisions affecting the target company

☑ Controlling interest

Holding a sufficiently large number of shares in a company so as to be able to control its prices.

☑ Convergence

Narrowing of the difference between the futures contract and the value of the underlying asset during the final days of the contract

☑ Conversion Price

The price at which a convertible instrument is converted into shares of the company.

☑ Conversion Ratio

The number of shares which may be acquired upon the conversion of a convertible instrument. The ratio is calculated as instrument's principal amount divided by conversion price.

☑ Convertible Bond

A bond giving the investor the option to convert the bond into equity at a fixed conversion price or as per a pre-determined pricing formula.

☑ Corners

A corner occurs when a person buys up a substantial volume of a security knowing that other market participants will be forced to buy from him at a higher price. An example of this would be when the other market participants hold short positions in the security which must be settled. A similar practice is the "abusive squeeze" where a person takes advantage of a shortage in an asset by controlling the demand side and creating artificial prices.

☑ Corporate Governance

The way in which companies run themselves, in particular the way in which they are accountable to those who have a vested interest in their performance, especially their shareholders.

☑ Corporate raiders

A cash rich person who may either by himself or through the company he controls buys in very large numbers of equity shares of a target company with a view to taking over that company.

☑ **Corporate restructuring**

Involves making radical changes in the composition of the businesses in the company's portfolio.

☑ **Correction**

Temporary reversal of trend in share prices. This could be a reaction (a decrease following a consistent rise in prices) or a rally (an increase following a consistent fall in prices).

☑ **Counter party risk**

The risk that between the time a transaction has been arranged and the time of actual settlement, the counterparty to the transaction will fail to make the appropriate payment.

☑ **Coupon**

The interest paid on a bond expressed as a percentage of the face value. If a bond carries a fixed coupon, the interest is paid on an annual or semi-annual basis. The term also describes the detachable certificate entitling the bearer to payment of the interest.

☑ **Coupon Rate**

The interest rate stated on the face of coupon.

☑ **Cover**

(1) To take out a forward foreign exchange contract.

(2) To close out a short position by buying the currency or securities which have been sold.

(3) To insure.

(4) The purchase or sale of futures to offset a previously established short or long position.

☑ Covered call option writing

A strategy in which one sells call options while simultaneously owning an equivalent position in the underlying security.

☑ Covered put option writing

A strategy in which one sells puts and simultaneously is short of an equivalent position in the underlying security.

☑ Covered warrant

A stock, basket, or index warrant issued by a party other than the issuer of the underlying stock(s) and secured by the warrant issuer's holding in the underlying securities or the warrant issuer's general credit standing.

☑ Credit rating

Credit ratings measure a borrower's creditworthiness and provide an international framework for comparing the credit quality of issuers and rated debt securities. Rating agencies allocate three kinds of ratings: issuer credit ratings, long-term debt, and short-term debt. Issuer credit ratings are amongst the most widely watched. They measure the creditworthiness of the borrower including its capacity and willingness to meet financial needs. The top credit rating issued by the main agencies – Standard & Poor's, Moody's and Fitch IBCA - is AAA or Aaa. This is reserved for a few sovereign and corporate issuers. Ratings are divided into two broad groups - investment grade and speculative (junk) grade.

☑ **Credit rating agency**

Credit rating agency means a body corporate which is engaged in, or proposes to be engaged in, the business of rating of securities offered by way of public or rights issue.

☑ **Credit Risk**

The risk that a counterparty will not settle an obligation for full value, either when due or at any time thereafter. Credit risk includes pre-settlement risk (replacement cost risk) and settlement risk (Principal risk).

☑ **Cross collateralization**

Practice of using assets as back up or secondary collateral for debt other than the debt they are primarily pledged for. A network of cross collateralization may facilitate an increase in borrowing or a reduction in borrowing cost.

☑ **Cross hedging**

Practice of altering the risk characteristic of a predetermined position in one cash good by taking out a position in a future or forward contract which is based on a good which differs significantly from that of the initial cash position.

☑ **Cross margining**

An arrangement between and among custodial and clearing organizations to partially offset excess risk-adjusted margin deposited with one entity against margin requirements with another.

☑ **Cross-Rate (U.S)**

The exchange rate between currencies A and C which is derived from the rate between A and B and the rate between B and C. Thus if $ 1 = DM 2.50 and $1=Yen 250, the cross rate between the DM and Yen is DM 1= Yen 100.

☑ **Cum**

Means 'with' A cum price includes the right to any declared dividend (cd) or bonus (cb).

☑ **Cumulative Convertible Preference Shares**

A type of preference shares where the dividend payable on the same accumulates, if not paid. After a specified date, these shares will be converted into equity capital of the company.

☑ **Cumulative Preference Shares**

A type of preference shares on which dividend accumulates if not paid. All arrears of preference dividend have to be paid out before paying dividend on equity shares.

☑ **Current Asset**

Cash or an item of value expected to be converted into cash within one year or one operating cycle, whichever is longer.

☑ **Current Liability**

Accounting term for money payable within the current accounting year, on account of trade creditors, taxation, dividends, etc. To these are often added provisions, i.e. any charges or liabilities (various government duties, disputed claims, etc.) which the company may have to settle within the accounting year.

☑ **Current Ratio**

Current ratio measures a company's current assets relative to its current liabilities. This gives an indication of its abilities to meet short-term liabilities; the higher the ratio, the more liquid the company.

☑ **Current Yield**

A measure of the return to a bondholder calculated as a ratio of the coupon to the market price. It is simply the annual coupon rate divided by the clean price of the bond.

☑ **Custodian**

An organization, usually a bank or any other approved institutions, that hold the securities and other assets of mutual funds and other institutional investors.

☑ **Custody risk**

The risk of loss of securities held in custody occasioned by the insolvency, negligence or fraudulent action of the custodian or of a sub-custodian.

☑ **Dabba trading**

Trading of securities outside the stock exchanges. The broker instead of routing the trade of his clients in the system of stock exchanges, matches or executes the trades of its clients in a system provided by him outside the stock exchange.

☑ **Daily Margin**

The amount that has to be deposited at the Stock Exchange on a daily basis for the purchase or sale of a security. This amount is decided by the stock exchange.

☑ **Daisy chain**

A kind of fictitious trading, or wash selling, whereby a group of unscrupulous investors artificially inflate the price of a security so that they sell it at a profit. As a stock price rises due to increased volume, investors who didn't do all their homework may be attracted to the stock in order to participate in the rising price. These investors are typically caught owning a stock that continues to depreciate long after the daisy chain sells out their positions for a profit.

☑ **Dalal Street**

Street on which The Stock Exchange, Mumbai is situated. Used synonymously for The Stock Exchange, Mumbai.

☑ **Dawn Raid (U.S.)**

A situation in which a predator broker sweeps into the market the instant it opens and buys up a large block of shares before the others have chance to react.

☑ **Day Order**

A day order is an order that remains good till the end of the trading day. If the Order does not perform by the time the market closes, the Order will be cancelled.

☑ **Day Trader**

A new breed of retail investor, found mostly in the United States who deals on the stock market via online brokers from dawn to dusk. A day trader undertakes many different buy and sell transactions during the day. Previously trading could only be carried out by stock broking professionals with access to expensive trading terminals. Day traders love the Internet–related dotcom stock and have been blamed for some of the volatility that these stocks have been prone to.

☑ **Dealer**

A firm that enters into transactions as a counterparty on both sides of the market in one or more products.

☑ **Debentures**

Bonds issued by a company bearing a fixed rate of interest usually payable half yearly on specific dates and principal amount repayable on a particular date on redemption of the debentures.

☑ **Debenture Trustee**

A trustee of a trust deed for securing any issue of debentures of a body corporate.

☑ **Deferred Futures**

The most distant months of futures contract.

☑ **Deferred net settlement**

A category of payments system in which banks continually send payment instructions over a period of time, with final transfer occurring at the end of the processing cycle. During the period, a record is kept of net debits and credits.

☑ **Defined Benefit Plan**

A pension plan in which the sponsor agrees to make specified payments to qualifying employees. The pension obligations are effectively the debt obligation of the plan sponsor.

☑ **Defined Contribution Plan**

A pension plan in which the sponsor is responsible only for making specified contributions into the plan on behalf of qualifying participants.

☑ **Delisting exchange**

The exchange from which securities of a company are proposed to be delisted in accordance with SEBI Delisting Guidelines.

☑ **Delisting of securities**

Permanent removal of securities of a listed company from a stock exchange. As a consequence of delisting, the securities of that company would no longer be traded at that stock exchange.

☑ **Delivery**

Presentation of securities with transfer deeds in fulfillment of a transaction.

☑ **Delivery Notice (U.S.)**

The written notice given by the seller of his intention to make delivery against an open short futures position on a particular date.

☑ **Delivery Order**

An output given to each member of the Stock Exchange at the end of a settlement period containing particulars such as number of shares, value of shares, names of the receiving members etc. To enable him to deliver such shares in time.

☑ **Delivery Price**

The price fixed by the Stock Exchange at which deliveries on futures are invoiced. Also the price at which the future contract is settled when deliveries are made.

☑ **Dematerialise**

The process of transforming securities holdings in physical form to those in electronic form through a Depository Participant.

☑ **Demutualization**

Process of transition from "mutually-owned" association to a company "owned by shareholders". In other words, transformation of the legal structure from a mutual form to a business corporation form and privatisation of the corporations so constituted, is referred to as demutualization.

☑ **Depository**

A system of organisation, which keeps records of securities, deposited by its depositors. The records may be physical or simply electronic records.

☑ **Depository participant (DP)**

An agent of the depository through which it interfaces with the investor. A DP can offer depository services only after it gets proper registration from SEBI.

☑ **Depreciation**

A fall in value of a security or security index or a currency in terms of others or its purchasing power.

☑ **Depth of Market**

The number of shares of a security that can be bought or sold at the best bid or offer price.

☑ **Deregulation**

The process of removing legal or quasi legal restriction on the type of business done or on the prices charged, within a particular industry. The aim of most deregulations is to increase competition by increasing the freedom of players in the industry.

☑ **Derivative Market**

Markets such as futures and option markets that are developed to satisfy specific needs arising in traditional markets. These markets provide the same basic functions as forward markets, but trading usually takes place on standardized contracts.

☑ **Derivative**

(1) A security derived from a debt instrument, share, loan whether secured or unsecured, risk instrument or contract for differences or any other form of security;

(2) A contract which derives its value from the prices, or index or prices, of underlying securities

☑ **Direct Quotation**

The quotation of variable units of domestic currency in terms of fixed units of foreign currency.

☑ **Dirty Float**

A floating security whose value is not solely determined by free market supply and demand pressures but also by interventions of the concerned authorities.

☑ Dirty Price

A price for a bond which includes the amount of interest that has accrued on the bond since the date of the last interest payment.

☑ Disclosure

Full and material information given by a company that may allow an investor to take an informed investment decision

☑ Discount

When a security is quoted at a price below its nominal or face value, it is said to be at a discount.

☑ Disintermediation

A situation where some intervention usually by government agencies for the purpose of controlling or regulating the growth of financial intermediaries lessens their advantage in the provision of financial services and drives financial transfers and businesses into other channels.

☑ Distribution

Return to investors of the accumulated income of a trust or mutual fund and distribution of capital gains.

☑ Distribution Analysis

A statement showing the pattern of holding of a security as on a given date.

☑ Distribution Dates

The dates on which income is paid to unit holders as in a trust, or mutual fund.

☑ Distribution Period

The period over which the income of a unit trust or mutual fund is accumulated before its distribution to investors.

☑ Diversification

Spreading the risk by constructing a portfolio that contains many different investments whose returns are relatively uncorrelated. Thus, risk levels can be reduced without a corresponding reduction in returns

☑ Dividend

A dividend means when the company earns profit, a particular portion of their earnings is distributed to shareholders or the people who own the company stock on a quarterly or annual basis. Not every company pays dividends, and if you're after penny stocks, you'll likely not get any dividends.

☑ Dividend Cover

Denotes the number of times equity earnings per share covers the equity dividend per share.

☑ Dividend Notification

A requirement that companies notify the Stock Exchange immediately that the company intends to declare dividend so that it can set the ex dividend date

☑ **Dividend Payable**

A current liability showing the amount due to stock holders/shareholders for dividend declared but not paid.

☑ **Don't Fight The Tape (U.S)**

Colloquial expression meaning, "Don't trade against the Market trend".

☑ **Dotcom Stocks**

Companies whose products or services are in some way dependent on the Internet and which have the suffix ".com" (dot.com) as part of their registered name.

☑ **Downside risk**

An estimate of the amount of loss the holder of a security might suffer if there is a fall in its value.

☑ **Dumping**

In the securities market the offering of large amounts of stock without regard for the effect on prices on the market. In the international trade, the selling of goods overseas below cost to get rid of a surplus or to gain a competitive edge over the foreign firms.

☑ **Dutch Auction**

An auction in which the auctioneer's prices fall rather than rise. In such an auction, the first person to bid wins whatever it is that the auctioneer is selling. The system is used in the Dutch flower markets and also, occasionally, as a method of selling securities.

☑ **EDGAR**

EDGAR (Electronic Data Gathering, Analysis and Retrieval System) is an electronic system formulated by Securities Exchange Commission, USA, which is used by companies to transmit documents required by SEC relating to corporate offerings and ongoing disclosure obligations.

☑ **EDIFAR**

EDIFAR is Electronic Data Information Filing and Retrieval system. Securities and Exchange Board of India (SEBI) in association with National Informatics Centre (NIC) has set up the EDIFAR to facilitate filing of certain documents/statements by the listed companies online on the Web site (www.sebi.gov.in). This would involve electronic filing of information in a standard format by the companies.

☑ **Effective Sale (U.S)**

A round lot transaction consummated on the floor of the New York Stock Exchange after entry of an odd-lot order by a customer. Its price is used to determine the execution price for odd-lot order after consideration of the dealers' fee.

☑ **Electronic fund transfer (EFT)**

System which utilizes computer and electronic components in order to transfer money or financial assets. EFT is information based and intangible.

☑ **Employee Stock Option**

"Employee stock option" means the option given to the whole-time directors, officers or employees of a company which gives such directors, officers or employees, the benefit or right to purchase or subscribe at a future date, the securities offered by the company at a predetermined price.

☑ **Employee Stock Purchase Scheme (ESPS)**

"Employee stock purchase scheme (ESPS)" means a scheme under which the company offers shares to employees as part of a public issue or otherwise.

☑ **Emerging Markets**

Term used to describe the financial markets of developing countries. Definitions vary of which countries are emerging and which are not. However, the emerging market indices compiled by the IFC and Morgan Stanley are often used as benchmarks.

☑ **Entry Fee**

Fee paid by an investor when purchasing units in a trust or managed fund. The fee is included in the price that new investors pay.

☑ **Equity**

The ownership interest in a company of holders of its common and preferred stock.

☑ **Equity premium**

The difference between the expected return from holding stock and from holding riskless bonds.

☑ **Equity Trust**

Unit Trust which invests mainly in equity shares with a component in cash and in fixed interest investment.

☑ **Escrow account**

The trust account established by a broker under the provisions of the license law for the purpose of holding funds on behalf of the broker's principal or some other person until the consummation or termination of a transaction.

☑ **Eurobond**

Eurobonds are issued in a specific currency outside the currency's domicile. They are not subject to withholding tax and fall outside the jurisdiction of any one country. The Eurobond market is based in London. Not to be confused with euro-denominated bonds.

☑ **Euroequities**

Equities underwritten and distributed to investors outside the country of origin of the issuer.

☑ **European Option**

A put or call that can be exercised only on its expiration date. The term has nothing to do with where the option is traded or what underlies it. Stock options listed on European option exchanges are usually American Style options in the sense that they can be exercised prior to the expiration date.

☑ **EVA**

Economic Value Added. Conceived by consultants Stern Stewart & Co, EVA is a popular method of measuring a company's profitability. EVA is calculated by taking the total cost of capital from post-tax operating profit.

☑ **Ex**

Means 'Without'. A price so quoted excludes recently declared dividends (xd) rights (xr) or bonus shares (xb).

☑ **Excess Spread Policy (U.S.)**

A NASD requirement that prohibits market makers from entering quotations in the NASDAQ system that exceed prescribed parameters for maximum allowable spreads.

☑ **Exchange**

Regulated market place where capital market products are bought and sold through intermediaries.

☑ **Exchange Rate Risk**

The risk that adverse movements in exchange rates lead to capital losses in assets or revaluation of liabilities.

☑ **Exchange-traded derivative**

A derivative which is listed and traded at an organised market-place. Derivatives exchanges generally provide standardised contracts and central clearing facilities for participants.

☑ **Exchange traded funds (ETF)**

A security that tracks an index but has the flexibility of trading like a stock.

☑ **External Commercial Borrowings**

In India External Commercial Borrowings are defined to include commercial bank loans, buyers' credit, suppliers' credit, securitised instruments such as Floating Rate Notes and Fixed Rate Bonds, etc., credit from official export credit agencies and commercial borrowings from the private sector window of Multilateral Financial Institutions such as International Finance Corporation (Washington), ADB, AFIC, CDC etc. ECBs are being permitted by the Government as a source of Finance for Indian corporates for expansion of existing capacity as well as for fresh investment.

☑ **Ex-Dividend Date**

The date on or after which the buyer of a security is not entitled to the dividend already declared.

☑ **Ex-Right Date**

The date on which the official quotation for a share is marked XR i.e. ex rights, in the daily official list.

☑ **Exit Fees**

Fees charged by mortgage trusts/mutual funds on a sliding scale as penalty for early withdrawal.

☑ **Expected Return**

The return an investor might expect on an investment if the same investment were made many times over an extended period. The return is found through the use of mathematical analysis.

☑ **Extrinsic Value**

The amount by which the market price of an option exceeds the amount that could be realized if the option were exercised and the underlying commodity liquidated. Also known as time value.

☑ **Face Value**

The value that appears on the face of the scrip, same as nominal or par value of share/debentures.

☑ **Family of Funds**

A group of mutual funds, each typically with its own investment objective, managed and distributed by the same company.

☑ **Feeder Fund**

Unit Trusts or Mutual Funds which invest in other trusts promoted by the same manager.

☑ **Fill or Kill (Fok) Order**

An order that requires the immediate purchase or sale of a specified amount of stock, though not necessarily at one price. If the order cannot be filled immediately, it is automatically cancelled (killed).

☑ **Financial crisis**

Sharp,brief,ultracyclical deterioration of all or most of a group of financial indicators – short term interest rates, asset (stock, real estate, land) prices, commercial insolvencies and failures of financial institutions.

☑ **Firewall**

A barrier designed to prevent losses or risks taken in one part of a financial institution from weakening other parts of institution.

☑ **Firm allotment**

Allotment on a firm basis in public issues by an issuing company made to Indian and multilateral development financial institutions ,Indian mutual funds , foreign institutional investors including non-resident Indians and overseas corporate bodies and permanent/regular employees of the issuer company.

☑ **First in/First out**

A popular inventory cost accounting procedure in which the first item manufactured is assumed to be the first one sold by the company

☑ **Five against bond spread**

A spread in the futures markets created by taking offsetting positions in futures contracts for five-year treasury bonds and long-term (15-30 year) treasury bonds.

☑ **Fixed Asset**

An item of value used in current operation that would normally be of use for more than one year.

☑ **Fixed Liability**

An obligation of a company payable more than a year hence.

☑ **Flip-Over**

A provision in a poison pill that gives shareholders the right to buy the company's shares (or the shares of the surviving company after a merger) at half price. Unlike a Flip-in, a flip-over right does not become effective simply because an interested shareholder buys some stock. Usually it becomes effective when (i) there is an interested shareholder and (ii) the company engages in certain transactions with the interested shareholder or an affiliate, such as a merger or a sale of all or a large part of its assets. Historically, the flip-over poison pill was devised several years before the more powerful flip-in. At that time the essential discrimination against the interested shareholder that the flip-in entails was widely considered illegal. Now the two are generally combined, although under most circumstances the flip-in provision of the pill dominates any potential bidder's attention.

☑ **Flip-in poison pill plan**

Shareholders are issued rights to acquire stock in the target at a significant discount which is usually 50%.

☑ **Flip-in**

The most important characteristic of the most effective rights plan (position pill) in use today. It gives shareholders the right to buy the company's shares at half price when someone becomes an 'interested shareholder', that is, crosses some stock ownership threshold such as 15% or 20%. The interested shareholder's rights are void. Other shareholders can (typically) use each of their rights to buy a number of shares equal to two times the exercise price (set in advance), divided by the current market price of the target company's stock. Usually, from the standpoint of a bidder, the flip-in right is a complete show stopper unless the bidder can convince a court that it should intervene. In the text we have tried to describe when courts intervene against poison pills under Delaware law.

☑ **Flip-over Poison Pill Plan**

The most popular type of poison pill anti-takeover defense. Shareholders of the target firm are issued rights to purchase common stock at an exercise price high above the current market price. If a merger occurs, the rights flip over and allow shareholders to purchase the acquiring firm's common stock at a substantial discount.

☑ **Float**

The number of shares issued and outstanding of a company's stock.

☑ **Floating rate coupon**

Coupon rate that varies with ("floats against") a standard market benchmark or index.

☑ **Floating Stock**

The fraction of the paid up equity capital of a company which normally participates in day to day trading.

☑ **Floor**

Trading hall of the Stock Exchange where transactions in securities take place. The trading ring where members and their assistants assemble with their order books for executing the order of their constituents.

☑ **Floor price**

The minimum offer price below which bids cannot be entered. The Issuer Company in consultation with the lead book runner fixes the floor price.

☑ **Flow back**

Securities recently placed in the markets that are resold on the issuers' national market. It is one of the major risks in an equity placement because it may frustrate the objective of internationalization of the equity market and cause downward pressure on its market price.

☑ **Foreign Exchange Rate**

The price of one currency in terms of the other.

☑ **Foreign institutional investor**

An institution established or incorporated outside India which proposes to make investment in India in securities; provided that a domestic asset management company or domestic portfolio manager who manages funds raised or collected or brought from outside India for investment in India on behalf of a sub-account, shall be deemed to be a Foreign Institutional Investor.

☑ **Fortune 500 (U.S.)**

Since 1958, Fortune Magazine has published a list of five hundred largest American Industrial Corporations, ranked according to size of sales.

☑ **Forward Contract**

An agreement for the future delivery of the underlying commodity or security at a specified price at the end of a designated period of time. Unlike a future contract, a forward contract is traded over the counter and its terms are negotiated individually. There is no clearing house for forward contracts, and the secondary market may be non-existent or thin.

☑ **Forward rate agreement:**

A forward contract on interest rates in which the rate to be paid or received on a specific obligation for a set period of time, beginning at some time in the future, is determined at contract initiation.

☑ **Free cash flow**

Calculated by adding depreciation to net income, and subtracting capital expenditures. Free cash flow represents the cash that is available for a company to spend after financing a capital project.

☑ **Free-rider Paradox**

Sometimes benefits and costs cannot be allocated accurately or at all to users by the markets or otherwise. A free rider tries to take advantage of this situation. The paradox is that if everyone tries to free ride no one can and everyone is worse off. An important example is the natural environment. Most industrial users of the natural environment are free riders. Everyone collectively is worse off but no one individually finds it worthwhile to stop. In takeovers, an important recent example is the basic research part of corporate research and development. It is impossible to limit the benefits from basic research to the corporation who pays the bill. Therefore, there will be a strong temptation for companies to free ride. Competition in the product and takeover market should increase this temptation.

☑ **Front Running**

An unethical practice where brokers trade an equity based on information from the analysis department before their clients have been given the information. Fund manager /broker buys or sells securities in advance of a substantial client order or whereby a futures or options position position is taken about an impending transaction in the same or related futures or options contract.

☑ Fund of funds

Fund of funds scheme means a mutual fund scheme that invests primarily in other schemes of the same mutual fund or other mutual funds.

☑ Fungible securities

Securities which are easily interchangeable with another in the same class.

☑ Futures Contract

An exchange traded contract generally calling for delivery of a specified amount of a particular financial instrument at a fixed date in the future. Contracts are highly standardized and traders need only agree on the price and number of contracts traded.

☑ Galla

Cutting in rates. It is the practice of depriving a client a higher rate while selling or lowest rate while buying over and above the brokerage.

☑ Garage (U.S)

One of the small trading areas just off the main trading floor of the New York Stock Exchange.

☑ Gilt Edged

A term used to describe a bond, generally issued by the Government or issued with a Government Guarantee so much so that there are no doubts about the ability of the issuer to pay regular interest and the principal amount to the bond holders.

☑ **Gilt fund**

Fund that invests exclusively in government securities.

☑ **GLOBEX**

A global after-hours electronic trading system.

☑ **Global Depository Receipts**

Any instrument in the form of a depository receipt or certificate (by whatever name it is called) created by the Overseas Depository Bank outside India and issued to non-resident investors against the issue of ordinary shares or Foreign Currency Convertible Bonds of issuing company.

☑ **Going Long**

Betting on the price of a stock that will increase so that you can buy at a low price and sell at a high price.

☑ **Golden Handcuffs (U.S)**

A contract between a broker and brokerage house, offering lucrative commissions, bonuses and other benefits as long as the broker stays with the firm. Upon leaving, the broker must return much of the compensation.

☑ **Golden Parachute (U.S.)**

A generous compensation contract awarded by the management to themselves in the anticipation of a takeover.

☑ **Golden Share**

A share with special voting rights that give it peculiar power vis-a-vis other share.The term applies particularly to share retained by a government after privatisation. If a government wishes to sell off a company in a sensitive industry (defence, say) and yet retain control, it can hold on to a golden share. This might give it the right to veto any takeover bid.

☑ **Good Delivery**

Proper delivery by a seller to the buyer of the securities without any defect so that they can be transferred without any additional documentation.

☑ **Goodwill**

The part of value of a business that is based on good customer relations, high employee morale and other factors.

☑ **Grave dancer**

An acquirer who searches for bargains often among companies in dire financial straits or in bankruptcy.

☑ **Greenmail**

Common practice in the United States in the merger-mad 1980s. Somebody buys a larger chunk of share in a company and threatens to make hostile bid for the company. To buy him off the company buys back the shares at a much higher price than the greenmailer paid for them. So disgusted were ordinary Americans with this practice that they passed legislation which imposed an onerous tax on any profit made from greenmail.

☑ **Green shoe option**

Green Shoe option means an option of allocating shares in excess of the shares included in the public issue and operating a post-listing price stabilizing mechanism in accordance with the specific provisions in DIP Guidelines, which is granted to a company to be exercised through a stabilising Agent

☑ **Grey Knight**

One who offers to buy shares of the bidding company as an aid to the defence.

☑ **Gross**

When used in connection with dividend or interest implies amount without any deduction of tax etc.

☑ **Gross spread**

The difference (spread) between a security's public offering price and the price paid to the issuer by an underwriter.

☑ **Growth Fund**

Unit trusts or Mutual Funds which invest with the objective of achieving mostly capital growth rather than income. Growth funds are mostly more volatile than conservative income or money market funds because managers invest on shares or property that are subject to larger price movements.

☑ **Guaranteed Coupon (GTD)**

Bonds issued by a subsidiary corporation and guaranteed as to principal and /or interest by the parent corporation.

☑ **Gun Jumping (U.S.)**

Illegally soliciting orders before SEC registration is effective. Buying a security based on information that is not yet public (inside information).

☑ **Haircut**
   1. The margin or more frequently, the capital tied up when a financial intermediary takes a position.
   2. A commission or fee for execution of a transaction (uncommon).

☑ **Hammering The Market**

Intensive sale of stocks to drive prices down.

☑ **Hand Delivery**

Delivery and payment on the date stipulated by the Stock Exchange.

☑ **Hedge**

An asset, liability or financial commitment that protects against adverse changes in the value of or cash flows from another investment or liability. An unhedged investment or liability is called an "exposure". A perfectly matched hedge will gain in value what the underlying exposure loses or lose what the underlying exposure gains.

☑ Hedge Funds

Private investment pools that invest aggressively in all types of markets, with managers of the fund receiving a percentage of the investment profits. The name is something of a misnomer since a hedge fund's raison d'etre is quite the opposite of hedging.

☑ Hedge Ratio

The proportion of one asset required to hedge against movements in the price of another.

☑ Herfindahl-Hirschman (HH) Index

The sum of the squares of the market shares of companies in any given industry. It is a measure of industry concentration and is more sensitive to the effects of mergers than simple market shares.

☑ Horizontal spread

The purchase of either a call or put option and the simultaneous sale of the same type of option with typically the same strike price but with a different expiration month. Also referred to as calendar spread.

☑ Hostile Bid

An effort to gain control of a target company that has not been agreed to by the target's management and board, usually through a tender offer or an unsolicited proposal to the board. Sometimes called an unsolicited bid.

☑ **Hot Issue**

A security that is expected to trade in the after market at a premium over the public offering price.

☑ **Hot Money**

Short term international capital movements, motivated by interest rate differential or revaluation hopes/ devaluation fears.

☑ **Hybrid**

Any security which has the character of more than one type of security, including their derivatives.

☑ **Hypothecation**

Pledging assets against a loan. The ownership of the asset or the income from the asset is not transferred, except that in default of repayment of loan the asset may be sold to realize its value. Brokers will accept shares as collateral for loans to finance purchase of shares or to cover short sales.

☑ **Implied Volatility**

The value of the price or rate volatility variable that would equate current option price and fair value. Alternatively, the value of the volatility variable that buyers and sellers appear to accept when the market price of an option is determined. Implied volatility is calculated by using the market price of an option as the fair value in an option model and calculating (by iteration) the volatility level consistent with that option price.

☑ Income Distribution

Distribution of income of a mutual fund to its unit holders, in proportion to the number of units held.

☑ Independent directors

Independent directors are directors who apart from receiving director's remuneration do not have any other material pecuniary relationship or transactions with the company, its promoters, its management or its subsidiaries, which in the judgement of the board may affect their independence of judgement

☑ Indexed asset

An indexed asset has coupon and principal payments that are adjusted upward in response to increase in price level. This adjustment is intended to compensate lenders for the decline in purchasing power of loan repayments.

☑ Index Fund

A mutual fund which invests in a portfolio of shares that matches identically the constituents of a well known stock market index. Hence changes in the value of the fund mirror changes in the index itself.

☑ Index futures

Futures contract based on an index, the underlying asset being the index, are known as Index Futures

Contracts. For example, futures contract on NIFTY Index and BSE-30 Index. These contracts derive their value from the value of the underlying index.

☑ Index option contracts

The options contracts, which are based on some index, are known as Index options contract. The buyer of Index Option Contracts has only the right but not the obligation to buy / sell the underlying index on expiry. Index Option Contracts are generally European Style options i.e. they can be exercised / assigned only on the expiry date.

☑ Index Trusts

Trust funds in which investment strategy involves mirroring particular share market or fixed interest market index.

☑ Indian Depository Receipt

A receipt, evidencing an underlying foreign security, issued in India by a foreign company which has entered into an agreement with the issuer and depository, custodian and depository or underwriters and depository, in accordance with the terms of prospectus or letter of offer, as may be prescribed.

☑ Initial margin

The initial amount which customers have to put in before taking up a futures contract to guarantee the transaction.

☑ Initial Public Offering (IPO)

The first public issue by a public limited company.

☑ Inside Quote (U.S.)

The highest bid and lowest ask prices among all the competing market makers in a security i.e. the best bid and offer prices.

☑ Insider

Any person who, is or was connected with the company or is deemed to have been connected with the company, and who is reasonably expected to have access, connection, to unpublished price sensitive information in respect of securities of a company, or who has received or has had access to such unpublished price sensitive information

☑ Insider trading

Practice of corporate agents buying or selling their corporation's securities without disclosing to the public significant information which is known to them but which has not yet affected the price.

☑ Institutional Investors

Organizations those invest, including insurance companies, depository institutions, pension funds, investment companies, and endowment funds.

☑ Institutionalization

The gradual domination of financial markets by institutional investors, as opposed to individual investors. This process has occurred throughout the industrialized world.

☑ **Interdelivery spread**

The purchase of one delivery month of a given futures contract and simultaneous sale of another delivery month of the same contract on the same exchange. Also called intramarket spread.

☑ **In-the-Money**

A call option is said be in the money when it has a strike price below the current price of the underlying commodity or security on which the option has been written. Likewise when a put option has a strike price above the current price it is said to be in-the-money.

☑ **Intangible Assets**

An item of value whose true worth is hard or almost impossible to determine such as goodwill reputation, patents and so on.

☑ **Interest rate agreement**

An agreement whereby one party, for an upfront premium, agrees to compensate the other at specific time periods if a designated interest rate (the reference rate) is different from a predetermined level (the strike rate).

☑ **Interest rate cap**

Also called an interest rate ceiling, an interest rate agreement in which payments are made when the reference rate exceeds the strike rate.

☑ **Interest rate differential**

The difference between the existing rate of interest and the rate for the term remaining, multiplied by the principal outstanding and the balance of the term.

☑ **Interest rate forward contracts**

Nonstandardised, non listed agreements typically bought and sold by individuals or corporations that are often connected by ongoing business relations.

☑ **Interest rate futures**

Financial futures that are considered to be primarily sensitive to interest rate movements.

☑ **Interest rate hedges**

Position designed to restrict losses that would occur from specific interest rate movements.

☑ **Interest rate swap**

Contract in which two parties agree to swap interest payments for a predetermined period of time – traded in the OTC market.

☑ **Interest Rate Risk**

The risk that movements in the interest rates may lead to a change in expected return.

☑ **Interim Dividend**

A dividend payment made during the course of a company's financial year. Interim dividend, unlike the final dividend, does not have to be agreed in a general meeting.

☑ **Internal Rate of Return (IRR)**

The rate at which future cash flows must be discounted in order to equal the cash cost of the investment.

☑ **Intra-Day Trading**

Intraday trading means buying and selling your desired stocks on the same day so that before trading hours get over, all your trading positions will be closed within the same day.

☑ **Investment banker**

Financial conglomerate which conducts a full range of investment related activities from advising clients on securities issues, acquisitions and disposal of businesses, arranging and underwriting new securities, distributing the securities etc.

☑ **Investment Company**

A corporation, trust or partnership that invests pooled unit holder/shareholder money in securities appropriate to the organization's objective. Mutual funds, close–ended funds and unit investment trusts are the three types of investment companies.

☑ **Investment Objective**

The goal that an investor and mutual fund pursue together, e.g. current income, long term capital growth etc.

☑ **Investment Profit**

Profit which results from the difference between the purchase and selling prices of a security. Trading profit is short term while investment profit is medium or long term.

☑ IPO

IPO means a private company is turning into a public company by issuing its shares to the public for the first time. In the case of an IPO, the investor can buy the shares directly from the company.

☑ ISIN

ISIN (International Securities Identification Number)A unique identification number allotted for each security in the depository system by SEBI.

☑ ISO 15022

Common messaging standard adopted for electronic trades under Straight through Processing (STP) system

☑ Issuer

An entity which is in the process of issuing its securities. Also known as the "Originator".

☑ Jitney

Describes a situation where one broker who has direct access to a stock exchange performs trades for a broker who does not have access. A fraudulent activity in the penny stock market. It occurs when two brokers work together by trading a stock back and forth to rack up commissions and give the impression of trading volume.For example, in the first definition, a small firm whose volume of business is not sufficient to maintain a trader on the exchange would give its orders to a large dealer for execution.In the second definition, jitney or "the jitney game" is basically the same thing as circular trading.

☑ **Jobber**

Member brokers of a stock exchange who specialize, by giving two way quotations, in buying and selling of securities from and to fellow members. Jobbers do not have any direct contact with the public but they serve the useful function of imparting liquidity to the market.

☑ **Jobbers Spread**

The difference between the price at which a jobber is prepared to sell and the price at which he is prepared to buy. A large difference reflects an imbalance between supply and demand.

☑ **Jumbo Bonds (U.S)**

A certificate of deposit issued by a bank or savings and loan association for a huge amount usually for a period of a year or less.

☑ **Junk Bond**

High yield bond issued by low rated companies.

☑ **Kerb Dealings/Khangi Bhao**

See Band Ke Bhao

☑ **Kapli**

A standard form used by the broker to inform the Stock Exchange of his transactions for the purpose of matching a settlement.

☑ **Killer Bees (U.S.)**

Law firms, proxy solicitors and public relations firm employed to help a company management fight off an unfriendly takeover.

☑ **Kiting**

The act of misrepresenting the value of a financial instrument for the purpose of extending credit obligations or increasing financial leverage. Kiting generally occurs when securities firms fail to deliver securities involved in buy and sell transactions in a timely manner (before the three-day settlement period). When this occurs, the firm failing to receive the securities is required to purchase the shortage on the open market and charge the delinquent firm any associated fees. The fraudulent act of kiting occurs when the firm fails to purchase the securities on the open market and maintains a short position, delays delivery, or takes part in transactions contrary to SEC regulations regarding the proper settlement of trades.

☑ **Kiss Principle (U.S)**

Advice given by old pros to neophyte brokers on how they should explain to investors such sophisticated investment concepts as options and arbitrage. Keep it simple, stupid.

☑ **Lagging indicators**

Market indicators showing the general direction of the economy and confirming or denying the trend implied by the leading indicators or concurrent indicators.

☑ **Lame Duck**

A defaulter on a Stock Exchange who is not able to meet his market commitment and financial obligations of his business.

☑ **LIBOR - London Interbank Offer Rate**

Often used as a basis for pricing Euroloans. LIBOR represents the interest rate at which first class banks in London are prepared to offer dollar deposits to other first class banks. There are a number of similar rates like HIBOR (Hong Kong Interbank Offer Rate); SIBOR (Singapore Interbank Offer Rate); TIBOR (Toronto Interbank Offer Rate).

☑ **Last In First Out - LIFO**

An inventory cost accounting procedure in which the last item manufactured is assumed to be the first one sold by the company.

☑ **Law of one price**

An economic rule stating that a given security must have the same price regardless of the means by which one goes about creating that security. This implies that if the payoff of a security can be synthetically created by a package of other securities, the price of the package and the price of the security whose payoff it replicates must be equal.

☑ Lay Off

The sell off by an issuer of any or all unsubscribed shares in a rights offering to the underwriters at the subscription price.

☑ Leading indicators

Market indicators that signal the state of the economy for the coming months.

☑ Lead Manager

The merchant banker(s) associated with the issue and responsible for due diligence and other associated issue related activities.

☑ Legal risk

The risk of loss because a law or regulation is applied in an unexpected way or because a contract cannot be enforced.

☑ Letter of offer

A letter of offer is a document addressed to the shareholders of the target company containing disclosures of the acquirer/ (Persons Acting in Concert) PACs, target company, their financials, justification of the offer price, the offer price, number of shares to be acquired from the public, purpose of acquisition, future plans of acquirer etc.

☑ **Leverage**

The use of borrowed money to finance an investment.

☑ **Leveraged Buyout**

The purchase of shares usually by the management of a company using its own assets as collateral for loans provided by banks or insurance company.

☑ **Liabilities**

Any claim for money against the assets of a company, such as bills of creditors, income tax payable, debenture redemption, interest on secured and unsecured loans, etc. Although on balance sheet shareholder's equity is shown under liability, it has no claim on the assets of a company, unless it goes into liquidation.

☑ **Limit Order**

A limit order is to buy shares below a fixed price and sell shares above a fixed price. It is advisable to use a limit order to trade shares.

☑ **Line Business**

Brokers who have teleprints in their office communicate the quantity, price etc., as soon as deals are struck, for onward transmission to their branch offices. This is known as line business. It also includes arbitrage.

☑ **Liquidation**

The process of converting stocks into cash. Also means the dissolution of a company.

☑ **Liquidity**

Liquidity means how stocks can be sold off quickly. Shares that get sold consist of high trade volumes quickly and are called highly liquid.

☑ **Liquidity Adjustment Facility (LAF)**

Under the scheme, repo auctions (for absorption of liquidity) and reverse repo auctions (for injection of liquidity) will be conducted on a daily basis (except Saturdays). It will be same-day transactions, with interest rates decided on a cut-off basis and derived from auctions on a uniform price basis.

☑ **Liquid Assets**

Proportion of listed unit trust's or mutual fund portfolio that is kept in cash or easily encashable assets to meet any request for redemption.

☑ **Liquidity Risk**

The risk that a solvent institution is temporarily unable to meet its monetary obligations.

☑ **Listed Company**

A company which has any of its securities offered through an offer document listed on a recognised stock exchange and also includes Public Sector

Undertakings whose securities are listed on a recognised stock exchange.

☑ Listing

Formal admission of a security into a public trading system

☑ Listing Agreement

An agreement which has to be entered into by companies when they seek listing for their shares on a Stock Exchange. Companies are called upon to keep the stock exchange fully informed of all corporate developments having a bearing on the market price of shares like dividend, rights, bonus shares, etc.

☑ Load

A sales charge assessed by certain mutual funds (load funds) to cover selling costs. A front end load is charged at the time of purchase. A back-end load is charged at the time of sale.

☑ Load fund

A Load Fund is one that charges a percentage of Net Asset Value (NAV) for entry or exit.

☑ Locked or Crossed Quotations (U.S)

A temporary condition, normally associated with fast-moving, active markets, where the asking price of one market maker in a given security is the same or lower than the bid price of another market maker, thereby producing locked or crossed markets respectively.

☑ Lock in Trade

A securities transactions in which all the terms and conditions to the transactions are irrevocably accepted by the buyer and seller.

☑ Long Position

A position showing a purchase or a greater number of purchases than sales in anticipation of a rise in prices. A long position can be closed out through the sale of an equivalent amount.

☑ Loss on Security Provisions

The risk that changes in security prices may lead to capital losses.

☑ LP (Liquidity Premium)

Additional return required to compensate investors for purchasing illiquid assets.

☑ MIT

Market if touched (MIT). A limit order that automatically becomes a market order if the price is reached.

☑ Maintenance Margin

The minimum margin that must be maintained on a futures contract.

☑ **Management Charge/Fees**

The amount a mutual fund pays to its investment adviser for services rendered, including management of the fund's portfolio.

☑ **Manipulation of financial markets**

Activities whose objective is to alter prices in financial markets through the use of techniques that result in unnatural market prices, often through the use of wash sales or reporting of fictional or apparent market prices.

☑ **Maple Leaf**

Debt warrants entitling the holder to purchase a Government of Canada Bond.

☑ **Margin**

An advance payment of a portion of the value of a stock transaction. The amount of credit a broker or lender extends to a customer for stock purchase.

☑ **Markdown**

A charge levied by a broker when buying securities on its own account from a customer. (These purchases as principals from customer take place at the best bid prices minus a commission equivalent to markdown).

☑ **Marked to market basis**

The process whereby the book value or collateral value of a security is adjusted to reflect current market value.

☑ Market Capitalisation

It simply means the value of a company according to the stock market. That is the current value of all the shares of a company put together.

☑ Market Maker

A member firm who give two way quotation for particular security (ies) and who is under an obligation to buy and sell them subject to certain conditions such as overall exposure, spread etc.

☑ Market Model

This relationship is sometimes called the single-index model. The market model says that the return on a security depends on the return on the market portfolio and the extent of the security's responsiveness as measured by beta (b). In addition, the return will also depend on conditions that are unique to the firm. Graphically, the market model can be depicted as a line fitted to a plot of asset returns against returns on the market portfolio.

☑ Market Order

A market order is an order to buy and sell shares at the market price. Several investors don't go with this Order because the trade price in the market order remains volatile.

☑ Market Price

The last reported sale price for an exchange traded security.

☑ Marketable Lot

A fixed minimum number, in which or in multiples of which, shares are bought and sold on the stock exchange. For shares whose face value is Rs. 10, the marketable or trading lot may be 50 or 100. For Rs. 100 shares the market lot is usually 5 or 10. Companies may, however, decide on other lots, such as 1 share for Rs. 500, although it is now rare. Any number of share less than the marketable lot makes an odd lot, difficult to buy and disadvantageous to sell. When companies issue bonus or rights shares in less than 1:1 ratio, odd lots are often the result.

☑ Marking Up Prices

Prices fixed by the Stock Exchange to facilitate settlement of bargains in the specified securities, particularly at the end of the settlement period.

☑ Mark to market margin (MTM)

Collected in cash for all Futures contracts and adjusted against the available Liquid Net worth for option positions. In the case of Futures Contracts MTM may be considered as Mark to Market Settlement.

☑ Marking Up Prices

Prices fixed by the Stock Exchange to facilitate settlement of bargains in the specified securities, particularly at the end of the settlement period.

☑ **Markup**

A charge levied by a broker when selling securities from its own account to a customer. These sales as principals to a customer take place at the best ask price plus a commission equivalent to markup.

☑ **Matched Transaction**

A check is carried out on the computer to find out whether purchases and sales as reported by the members match. The transactions, thus compared are called matched transactions.

☑ **Maturity (Date)**

The date on which a loan, bond, or debenture becomes due for payment.

☑ **Maturity Value**

The amount an investor receives when a security is redeemed at maturity not including any periodic interest payments. The value usually equals the par value although on zero coupon, compound interest and multiplier bonds, the principal amount of the security at issuance plus the accumulated investment return on the security is included.

☑ **Merchant Banker**

Any person who is engaged in the business of issue management either by making arrangement regarding selling, buying or subscribing to securities or acting as manager, consultant, adviser or rendering corporate advisory service in relation to such issue management.

☑ Merger

The non-hostile and voluntary union of two companies.

☑ MIBOR

Mumbai Interbank Bid and Offer rates. Calculated by the average of the interbank offer rates based on quotations at nearly 30 major banks.

☑ Microcap fraud

Microcap fraud typically takes one of the two forms. The first – the pump and dump scheme – often involves fraudulent sales practices, including pressure tactics from boiler room operations where a small army of sales personnel could call potential investors using scrips to induce them to purchase house stocks - stocks in which the firm makes a market or has large inventory. The information conveyed to investors often is at best exaggerated and at worst completely fabricated. Increasingly these stocks are being touted on the internet by unregistered promoters. The promoters of these companies, and often company insiders, typically hold large amounts of stock and make substantial profits when the stock price rises following intense promotional efforts. Once the price rises, insider and brokers sell, realizing their profits. Second as part of pump and dump, unscrupulous brokers often employ a variety of fraudulent sales practices including bait and switch tactics, unauthorized trading, no net sales policies and churning.

☑ **Money laundering**

Process of converting the proceeds of illegal activities – disclosure of which would trigger financial losses or criminal prosecution – into real or financial assets whose origins remain effectively hidden from law enforcement officials and from society in general.

☑ **Money Market**

The market encompassing the trading and issuance of short-term non-equity debt instruments, including treasury bills, commercial paper, bankers' acceptance, certificates of deposits etc. The market may be local or international.

☑ **Money market mutual funds**

Schemes investing exclusively in safer short-term instruments such as treasury bills, certificates of deposit, commercial paper and inter-bank call money, government securities, etc.

☑ **Mortgage backed securities**

Securities backed by mortgage loans, including pass-through securities, modified pass-through securities, mortgage-backed bonds, and mortgage pay-through securities.

☑ **Mortgage Trust**

Unit trust which invests in mortgage loans. Effectively the unit trust invests money in real estate and receives an interest return with security over the property which has been purchased. The interest which is charged on mortgage trust loans is normally higher than that other sources of finance like banks so that the investor usually receives a very competitive rate or return.

☑ **Moral Hazard**

The risk that a party to a transaction has not entered into a contract in good faith has provided misleading information about its assets, liabilities or credit capacity or has an incentive to take unusual risks in a desperate attempt to avoid losses.

☑ **Moving Average**

The average of security or commodity prices over a period of few days or up to several years showing the trends up to the last interval. Each time the average is taken , the oldest price is dropped and the latest price is added. Thus the average is moving one.

☑ **Multilateral netting**

Multilateral netting is an arrangement among three or more parties to net their obligations. In settlement systems of this type transfers are irrevocable, but are only final after the completion of end-of-daysettlement.

☑ **Mutual Funds /Unit Trusts**

Mutual Fund is a mechanism for pooling the resources by issuing units to the investors and investing funds in securities in accordance with objectives as disclosed in offer document. A fund established in the form of a trust to raise monies through the sale of units to the public or a section of the public under one or more schemes for investing in securities, including money market instruments

☑ **NASDAQ (U.S.)**

Acronym for the National Association of Security Dealers Automated Quotations. This is an organization that does exactly what its name stands for. The system provides a computerized information network through which brokers, banks and other investment professionals can obtain upto the minute price quotations on securities traded over the counter.

☑ **Naked Option**

An option that is written without corresponding security or option position as protection in seller's account.

☑ **Narrowing the Spread**

The action taken by broker /dealer to narrow the spread between bids and offers by bidding higher or offering lower than the previous bid or offer. Also called closing the market.

☑ **National best bid and offer**

A term applying to the SEC requirement that brokers must guarantee customers the best available ask price when they buy securities and the best available bid price when they sell securities.

☑ Negotiated Dealing System (NDS)

Electronic platform for facilitating dealing in Government Securities and Money Market Instruments, introduced by RBI.

☑ Net Dividend

Dividend after deduction of tax payable from gross dividend

☑ Net Liquid Assets

Cash and readily marketable securities minus current liabilities of a company. This is the strictest test of a company's ability to meet current debt obligations.

☑ Netting

A system whereby outstanding financial contracts can be settled at a net figure, i.e. receivables are offset against payables to reduce the credit exposure to a counterparty and to minimize settlement risk.

☑ Net Working Capital

The excess of current assets over current liabilities.

☑ Net worth

The aggregate value of the paid up equity capital and free reserves (excluding reserves created out of revaluation), reduced by the aggregate value of accumulated losses and deferred expenditure not written off, including miscellaneous expenses not written of.

☑ **New Issue**

Shares of a company offered to the public, through a public issue, for the first time to be listed on the Stock Exchange.

☑ **Net Asset Value (NAV)**

The current market worth of a mutual fund's share. A fund's net asset value is calculated by taking the fund's total assets, securities, cash and any accrued earnings, deducting liabilities, and dividing the remainder by the number of units outstanding.

☑ **Net Option Value**

The difference between long option value (LOV) and short option value (SOV).

☑ **Net Realizable Value**

The current market price of an asset after deducting the costs of selling it.

☑ **Nifty**

The Nifty 50 Index, called the National Stock Exchange of India, is the primary and brad based stock market index for the equity market of India. The Nifty 50 consists of 50 Indian company stocks in 12 different sectors, and it is one out of two stock indices that are mainly used in the stock market.

☑ **Noise trading**

People who trade on noise are willing to trade even though from an objective point of view they would be better off by not trading. Perhaps they think the noise they are trading on is information or perhaps they just like to trade.

☑ No-action Letter

A form of written advice given by the staff of the SEC to lawyers. It is given in response to a request letter and is limited to the facts of a particular proposed undertaking. Generally, the advice concerns an ambiguity or apparently illogical result under the SEC laws or rules. If the request is granted, the staff says that, based upon the facts described, it (the staff) would not recommend that the Commission take any action against the conduct described. In theory, grant of a no-action letter does not foreclose private lawsuits or even prevent some action by the Commission itself. However, in practice the letter generally would be given great weight by a court.

☑ Non deliverable swap

Similar to a non deliverable forward, the only difference being that settlement for both parties is done through a major currency.

☑ Non Discriminatory Poison Pill

Anti-takeover defense plans which do not penalize acquirers exceeding a given shareholding limit. Include flip-over plans, preferred stock plans and ownership flip-in plans which permit cash offers for all shares.

☑ **No load fund**

A no-load fund is one that does not charge for entry or exit. It means the investors can enter the fund/ scheme at net asset value (NAV) and no additional charges are payable on purchase or sale of units.

☑ **Odd Lot**

Anything less than the standard unit of trading.

☑ **Off Balance Sheet Risk**

Risk relative to operations that are not reflected in variation of the institutions assets or liabilities, when undertaken, but are reflected when profit or loss occurs.

☑ **Offer Document**

As per SEBI DIP guidelines, offer document means Prospectus in case of a public issue or offer for sale and Letter of Offer in case of a rights issue.

☑ **Offer For Sale**

An offer of securities by existing shareholder(s) of a company to the public for subscription, through an offer document.

☑ **Offer period**

The period between the date of entering into Memorandum of Understanding or the public announcement, as the case may be and the date of completion of offer formalities relating to the offer.

☑ **Offer Price**

Price at which units in trust can be bought. It often includes an entry fee. It also refers to the price at which securities are offered to the public.

☑ **Ombudsman**

An independent person appointed to hear and act upon citizen's complaint about government services. Invented in Sweden, the idea has been widely adopted. For example, groups of banks, mortgage lenders and insurance companies in various countries have appointed ombudsmen to attend to the complaints of their customers. Customers who use the ombudsman's (free) service retain their full right to take legal action should they not agree with the ombudsman's decision .

☑ **Open ended scheme**

An open-ended fund or scheme is one that is available for subscription and repurchase on a continuous basis.

☑ **Open interest**

The number of contracts outstanding for a given option or futures contract.

☑ **Open market operation**

Purchase or sale of government securities by the monetary authorities (RBI in India) to increase or decrease the domestic money supply.

☑ **Open Order**

An order to buy and sell a security that remains in effect until it is either cancelled by the customer or executed.

☑ **Opening Price**

The rate at which the first transaction in a security is struck after the opening of the market.

☑ **Operating Income**

Net Sales less cost of sales, selling expenses, administrative expenses and depreciation. The pre-tax income from normal operations.

☑ **Operational risk**

The risk that deficiencies in information systems or internal controls could result in unexpected losses.

☑ **Option**

The contractual right, but not obligation, to buy (call option) or sell (put option) a specified amount of underlying security at a fixed price (strike price) before or at a designated future date (expiration date). The option writer is the party that sells the option. As per the Securities Contract Regulation Act (SCRA), "option in securities" means a contract for the purchase or sale of a right to buy or sell, or a right to buy and sell, securities in future, and includes a teji, a mandi, a teji mandi, a galli, a put, a call or a put and call in securities.

☑ **Option premium**

The market price of an option that is paid by an option buyer to the option writer (seller) for the right to buy (call) or sell (put) the underlying security at a specified price (called "strike price" or "exercise price") by the option's expiration date.

☑ **Option Seller**

Also called the option writer, the party who grants a right to trade a security at a given price in the future.

☑ **Option spread**

A spread is a type of option position where you buy an option and sell an option and both of them are from the same option class.

☑ **Optional Redemption**

An optional call provision reserved by the issuer that becomes exercisable after a certain number of years from issue date. This provision allows the clean up of small amounts of remaining principal with thin marketability.

☑ **Order**

Order means the purpose of buying and selling shares in a given range of price. For example, you have placed an order to buy 200 shares from company A, at a maximum price of Rs 50 per share.

☑ **Order book**

It is an 'electronic book' that shows the demand for the shares of the company at various prices.

☑ **Original Plan Poison Pill**

Also called preferred stock plan. An early poison pill antitakeover defense in which the firm issues a dividend of convertible preferred stock to its common stockholders. If an acquiring firm passes a trigger point of share ownership, preferred stockholders (other than the large block holder) can put the preferred stock to the target firm (force the firm to redeem it) at the highest price paid by the acquiring firm for the target's common or preferred stock during the past year. If the acquirer merges with the target, the preferred can be converted into acquirer voting stock with a market value no less than the redemption value at the trigger point.

☑ **OTC (Over the Counter)**

A financial transaction that is not made on an organised exchange. Generally the parties must negotiate all the details of each transaction or agree to use simplifying market conventions.

☑ **Out of the money option**

An option is described as being out of the money when the current price of the underlying is below the strike or exercise price for a call, and above the strike price for a put. Options can also be described as being deep out of the money when they are likely to expire out of the money.

☑ **Overtrading**

A broker/dealer overpays a customer for a security to enable the customer to subscribe to another security offered by that broker/dealer at a higher markup than the loss to be sustained when the firm sells the customer's first security at prevailing market prices.

☑ **Ownership Flip-in Plan**

A poison pill anti-takeover defense often included as part of a flip-over plan. Target stockholders are issued rights to purchase target shares at a discount if an acquirer passes a specified level of share ownership. The acquirer's rights are void and his or her ownership interest becomes diluted.

☑ **Paid in Capital**

The difference between par or book-keeping, value of a security and the amount realized from the sale or distribution of those shares by the company.

☑ **Paid up Capital**

The amount of capital, both equity and preference, paid up by the shareholders against the capital subscribed to by them.

☑ **Paper Profits/Paper Loss**

Unrealized profit/loss that exist only on paper because the investor has not finalized the transaction by actually selling the securities.

☑ **Par Value**

Means the face value of securities.

☑ **Pari Passu**

A term used to describe new issue of securities which have same rights as similar issues already in existence.

☑ Partial Tender Offer

A tender offer for less than all target shares; specifies a maximum number of shares to be accepted, but does not announce bidder's plans with respect to the remaining shares.

☑ Participating Preference Shares

The right of certain preference shareholders to participate in profits after a specified fixed dividend contracted for is paid. Participation right is linked with the quantum of dividend paid on the equity shares over and above a particular specified level.

☑ Partly Paid

Shares on which full nominal value has not been called up.

☑ Pay In/Pay Out

The days on which the members of a Stock Exchange pay or receive the amounts due to them are called pay in or pay out days respectively.

☑ Payment netting

Settling payments due on the same date and in the same currency on a net basis.

☑ Penny Stocks (U.S.)

Generic term for very low priced stocks- sometimes selling at a few pennies per share sometimes for a dollar or two- in speculative companies.

☑ **Persons acting in concert (PAC)**

Individual(s) /company(ies)/ any other legal entity(ies) who are acting together for a common objective or for a purpose of substantial acquisition of shares or voting rights or gaining control over the target company pursuant to an agreement or understanding whether formal or informal.

☑ **Pig**

Operators who get killed by the speculators.

☑ **Pink Sheets**

Listing of Over the Counter Stocks, the dealers who trade them and the prices at which these dealers are willing to buy and sell. Printed daily on loud pink newsprint and found in brokerage house and many banks.

☑ **Placing Power**

The ability of the financial institutions to place securities with the investor.

☑ **Plain vanilla transactions**

The most common and generally the simplest types of derivatives transaction. Plain vanilla is a relative concept, and no precise list of plain vanilla transactions exists. Transactions that have unusual or less common features are often called exotic or structured.

☑ Players

A diverse range of intermediaries and institutional investors active in the capital market. This includes securities firms, broker dealers, commercial banks, merchant banks, unit trust/mutual fund etc.

☑ Poison Pill (U.S.)

A defence technique when a company issues to its shareholders a special preferred dividend stock which is convertible, after a takeover, into the acquirer's shares. The successful bidder thus faces the prospect of heavy dilution.

☑ Poison Put

A provision in some new bond issues designed to protect bondholders against takeover-related credit deterioration of the issuer. Following a triggering event, bond holders may put their bonds to the corporation at an exercise price of 100-101 percent of the bond's face amount.

☑ Ponzi Scheme

A classic contrick that has been repeated many times both before and since Charles(Carlo) Ponzi gave it its name in the 1920s. The scheme begins with a crook setting up as a deposit taking institution. The crook invites the public to place deposits with the institution, and offers them a generous rate of interest. The interest is then paid out of new depositors' money, and the crook lives well off the old deposits. The whole scheme collapses when there are not enough new deposits coming in to cover the interest payment due on the old ones. By that time the modern day Ponzi hopes to be living under an alias in a hot country with few extradition laws.

☑ Pooling

The basic concept behind mutual funds in which a fund aggregates the assets of investors who share common financial goals. A fund uses the investment pool to buy a diversified portfolio of investments and each mutual fund share purchased represents ownership in all the funds underlying securities.

☑ Pools

A pool is essentially the same type of practice as a matched order, but involves more than one person colluding to generate artificial market activity.

☑ Poop and scoop

A highly illegal practice occurring mainly on the Internet A small group of informed people attempt to push down a stock by spreading false information and rumors. If they are successful, they can purchase the stock at bargain prices.

☑ Portfolio

The portfolio is a collection of all the investments that an investor has made right from purchasing a share for the first time.

☑ Portfolio investment

Investment which goes into the financial sector in the form of treasury bonds and notes, stocks, money market placements, and bank deposits. Portfolio investment involves neither control of operations nor ownership of physical assets.

☑ Portfolio manager

Any person who pursuant to a contract or agreement with a client ,advises or directs or undertakes on behalf of the client (whether as discretionary portfolio manager or otherwise) the management or administration of a portfolio of securities or the funds of the client as the case may be.

☑ Portfolio Turnover

A measure of the trading activity in a funds investment portfolio – how often securities are bought and sold by a fund.

☑ Position limit

The maximum number of listed option contracts on a single security which can be held by an investor or group of investors acting jointly.

☑ Position netting

The netting of payment instructions in respect of obligations between two or more parties, but which neither satisfies nor discharges those original obligations.

☑ Position trading

Type of trading involving the holding of open positions for an extended period of time.

☑ **Preferred Stock / Preference Shares**

Owners of this kind of stock are entitled to a fixed dividend to be paid regularly before dividend can be paid on common stock .They also exercise claims to assets, in the event of liquidation, senior to holders of common stock but junior to bondholders. Holders of preferred stock normally do not have a voice management.

☑ **Preferential allotment**

Further issue of shares / securities convertible into equity shares at a later date, to a select group of persons in preference to all the existing shareholders of the company.

☑ **Premium**

If an investor buys a security for a price above its eventual value at maturity he has paid a premium for it.

☑ **Price Band**

The range within which the price of a security or the index of a currency is permitted to move within a given period.

☑ **Price discovery**

A general term for the process by which financial markets attain an equilibrium price, especially in the primary market. Usually refers to the incorporation of information into the price

☑ **Price Earning Ratio**

The ratio of the market price of the share to earnings per share. This measure is used by investment experts to compare the relative merits of a number of securities.

☑ **Price rigging**

When persons acting in concert with each other collude to artificially increase or decrease the prices of a security, the process is called price rigging.

☑ **Price sensitive information**

Any information which relates directly or indirectly to a company and which if published is likely to materially affect the price of securities of the company.

☑ **Prime Rate**

The interest rate on loans, which a bank is charging its best, most credit-worthy business customers. This interest rate affects all borrowers - not merely those who actually pay the prime rate because the level of the prime rate and the direction in which it is moving tend to determine other interest rates.

☑ **Profit Taking**

Realizing profits by closing out an existing position

☑ **Programme Trading**

A technique, which uses decision rules, usually programmed on a computer, to generate trading decisions automatically.

☑ **Proprietary Fund (sub account)**

A fund where in the ownership of the funds is that of the Foreign Institutional Investor.

☑ **Prospectus**

Any document described or issued as a prospectus and includes any notice, circular, advertisement or other document inviting deposits from the public or inviting offers from the public for the subscription or purchase of any shares in, or debentures of, a body corporate.

☑ **Proxy**

One who votes for and on behalf of a shareholder at a company meeting.

☑ **Proxy Battle**

A battle between a company and some of its own shareholders. It starts with a group of dissident shareholders soliciting proxies in order to force through a shareholder resolution.

☑ **Public Announcement**

A public announcement is an announcement made in the newspapers by the acquirer primarily disclosing his intention to acquire shares of the target company from existing shareholders by means of an open offer.

☑ **Public Issue**

An invitation by a company to public to subscribe to the securities offered through a prospectus.

☑ **Public Securities Trust**

Pooled unit trust which invest unit holders money in government and semi government securities.

☑ **Puffing advertisement**

Advertising or planting some news in the newspaper or in any media in respect of a proposed corporate action and later taking the stand that the Board of directors did not approve the proposed corporate action or news about financial results, given in misleading or distorted manner intended to generate or induce trading in the scrip.

☑ **Pump and dump**

A highly illegal practice occurring mainly on the internet. A small group of informed people buy a stock before they recommend it to thousands of investors. The result is a quick spike in the price followed by an equally quick downfall. The people who have bought the stock early sell off when the price peaks.

☑ **Put-Call Parity Relationship**

The relationship between the price of a put and price of a call on the same underlying with the same expiration date, which prevents arbitrage opportunities.

☑ **Put Option**

An option that gives the right to sell a fixed number of securities at a specified price (the strike price) within a specified period of time.

☑ **Quotation (U.S)**

The NASD requirement that a market maker who receives order from another broker dealer executes the order at its displayed price on NASDAQ for the normal unit of trading or its displayed size, whichever is greater.

☑ **Quote**

The stock's latest trading prices contain information that is given in a quote. Sometimes, the quote is delayed by 20 minutes unless you're an actual stockbroker working in an existing trading platform.

☑ **Radar Alter (U.S)**

Close watch by a company's top executive on trading their company's stock. The objective is to detect any unusual amount of buying which might indicate that some one is attempting to acquire a chunk of the stock in anticipation of a takeover attempt.

☑ **Random Walk Theory**

Claims that a stock's past price action is no guide to future prices because prices move randomly, not in a pattern. Random walk theoreticians would sneer at the idea that because a stock has been moving up during the last few weeks it is likely to continue moving up.

☑ Real Time Gross Settlement (RTGS)

Concept designed to achieve sound risk management in the settlement of interbank payments. Transactions are settled across accounts held at the Central Bank on a continuous gross basis where settlement is immediate, final and irrevocable.

☑ Record Date

A date on which the records of a company are closed for the purpose of determining the stockholders to whom dividends, proxies rights etc., are to be sent.

☑ Red Herring

A preliminary prospectus filed with the Securities and Exchange Commission in the United States in order to test the market's reaction to a proposed new issue of securities. In Indian scenario, Red Herring is a draft prospectus which is used in book built issues. It contains all disclosures except the price and is used for testing the market reaction to the proposed issue.

☑ Redemption Price

The price at which a bond is redeemed.

☑ Registered Bonds

A bond which is registered in the books of the company in the name of the owner.

☑ Registrar to an issue

The person appointed by a body corporate or any person or group of persons to carry on the activities of collecting applications from investors in respect of an issue; keeping a proper record of applications and monies received from investors or paid to the seller of the securities and assisting body corporate or person or group of persons in- determining the basis of allotment of securities in consultation with the stock exchange; finalising of the list of persons entitled to allotment of securities; processing and despatching allotment letters, refund orders or certificates and other related documents in respect of the issue.

☑ **Regulation T/Regulation U (U.S)**

Two Federal Board regulations controlling respectively, the amount of credit a broker or a bank can extend to a client to buy securities. During recent years, under Regulation T (applying to Brokers), the Federal Reserve Board has set margin requirements on most stock at 50 per cent, meaning that the broker can lend a client no more than 50 per cent of the stocks he wishes to purchase. Regulation U applies in similar manner to banks.

☑ **Regulatory arbitrage**

A financial contract or a series of transactions undertaken, entirely or in part, because the transaction(s) enable(s) one or more of the counterparties to accomplish a financial or operating objective which is unavailable to them directly because of regulatory obstacles.

☑ **Rematerialisation**

The process of converting electronic holdings into physical securities through a Depository Participant.

☑ **Repurchase Agreement (repo)**

A financing arrangement used primarily in the government securities market whereby a dealer or other holder of government securities sells the securities to a lender and agrees to repurchase them at an agreed future date at an agreed price which will provide the lender an extremely low risk return. Repos are popular because they can virtually eliminate credit problems. The repo market is enlarged and enhanced by its use in federal board open market operations in the United States. Repos operate slightly differently in other markets.

☑ **Repurchase price**

The price or net asset value at which an open-ended scheme purchases or redeems its units from the unit holders. It may include exit load, if applicable.

☑ **Reverse book building**

Reverse book building is similar to the process of book building, which is aimed at securing the optimum price for a company's share. In reverse book building the investors' aim is to sell the shares to exit the company.

☑ **Reverse repo**

The purchase of securities with an agreement to resell them at a higher price at a specific future date. This is essentially just a loan of the security at a specific rate. Also called reverse repurchase agreement.

☑ **Rigged Market**

Manipulation of share price to attract buyers and sellers to the riggers advantage.

☑ **Rights Issue/ Rights Shares**

The issue of new securities to existing shareholders in a fixed ratio to those already held.

☑ **Rolling settlement**

The practice on many stock markets of settling a transaction a fixed number of days after the trade is agreed.

☑ **Ruling Price**

The current market price of a security.

☑ **Run**

A run involves a person creating activity in a security by successively buying or selling that security. The intention is that the increased activity would, in case where the person is buying, attract others to buy and push up the price. At that point, those organizing the run would then attempt to sell out at a financial gain. This is sometimes known as "pumping and dumping."

☑ **SEC (U.S.)**

Securities and Exchange Commission (SEC) The US Government agency that regulates securities trading. It has civil enforcement powers only and must seek criminal prosecution through the US Justice Department.

☑ **SIPC (Pronounced 'Si-Pick') (U.S.)**

Acronym for the Securities Investor Protection Corporation, a corporation created by Congress (although not a government agency) which will provide funds to protect investors cash and stocks left with brokers who are covered by SIPC should the brokerage firm fail. There are, however, definite limits to the amounts SIPC will provide and to the circumstances under which such payments will be made.

☑ **Safe Harbor (U.S.)**

Another way of fighting off an unfriendly takeover by a company. Here, the company that is the object of the takeover goes out and buys a radio station, airline, or similar business, under the assumption that ownership of a subsidiary in such a heavily regulated industry will make acquisition of the company less attractive.

☑ **Samurai Bonds**

Foreign bonds offered in the Japanese Bond Market.

☑ **Saturday Night Special (U.S.)**

A surprise tender offer with a 7-10 day expiration period. So called because the strategy often involves announcing it over the weekend, thus denying the rival management time to respond.

☑ **Sauda Book**

Members and authorized assistants are given a book called "Sauda Book" to record transactions of sales and purchases.

☑ **Scorched Earth Policy (U.S.)**

Extreme defence tactics by a defending company taking on heavy debt or selling off the key assets to save itself, to ward off a takeover.

☑ **Screen based trading**

Form of trading that uses modern telecommunication and computer technology to combine information transmission with trading in financial markets.

☑ **Sector fund**

A fund that invests primarily in securities of companies engaged in a specific investment segment. Sector funds entail more risk, but may offer greater potential returns than funds that diversify their portfolios.

☑ **Secondary Market**

The market for previously issued securities or financial instruments.

☑ **Secondary Sharing**

It is another offering used to sell more stocks and gain more money from the public.

☑ **Securities Lending Scheme**

A scheme formed in 1997 for lending of securities through an approved intermediary to a borrower under an agreement for a specified period with the condition that the borrower will return equivalent securities of the same type or class at the end of the specified period along with the corporate benefits accruing on the securities borrowed.

☑ **Securitization**

The process of homogenizing and packaging financial instruments into a new fungible one. Acquisition, classification, collateralization, composition, pooling and distribution are functions within this process.

☑ **SEDAR**

An electronic filing system (the System for Electronic Document Analysis Retrieval) in Canada that enables companies to file prospectuses and continuous disclosure documents.

☑ **Self clearing member**

A member of a clearing corporation or clearing house of the derivatives exchange or derivatives segment of a stock exchange who may clear and settle transactions on its own account or on account of its clients only and shall not clear or settle transactions in securities for any other trading members.

☑ **Selling Short**

A manner in which an investor sells securities he does not posses in the hope of buying them back later at a lower price.

☑ **Sensitive Index**

A share price index based on 30 active scrips developed by the Bombay Stock Exchange with 1978-79 as the base year.

☑ **Sensex**

Sensex is a figure that indicates all the relative share prices that are listed on the Bombay Stock Exchange.

☑ **Settlement Date**

The date specified for delivery of securities between securities firms.

☑ **Settlement Period**

For administrative convenience, a Stock Exchange divides the year into a number of settlement periods so as to enable members to settle their trades. All transactions executed during the settlement period are settled at the end of the settlement period.

☑ **Settlement risk (principal risk)**

The risk that the seller of a security or funds delivers its obligation but does not receive payment or that the buyer of a security or funds makes payment but does not receive delivery. In this event, the full principal value of the securities or funds transferred is at risk.

☑ **Share Market**

A share market is a market in which shares of a particular company are purchased and sold. The stock market is a definite example of a share market.

☑ **Share transfer agent**

Any person, who on behalf of any body corporate maintains the record of holders of securities issued by such body corporate and deals with all matters connected with the transfer and redemption of its securities. It can also be a department or division (by whatever name called) of a body corporate performing the above activities if, at any time the total number of the holders of securities issued exceed one lakh.

☑ **Shark Repellent (U.S.)**

Special provisions in a company's charter or bylaws designed to deter bidders.

☑ **Shelf Registration (U.S.)**

Here a company wishing to sell new stocks or bonds to the public can file a single plan with the Securities and Exchange Commission, outlining its intentions to sell such securities over the next two years. Once the plan – called a registration statement – has been filed and is sitting on the shelf at the SEC, the company may then sell all or part of the securities, without any further procedures, at any time it feels market conditions are right.

☑ **Short Covering**

Buying of stocks by a seller to complete his previous commitments.

☑ **Short position**

In futures, the short has sold the commodity or security for future delivery; in options, the short has sold the call or the put and is obligated to take a futures position if he or she is assigned for exercise.

☑ **Short squeeze**

A situation in which a lack of supply and an excess demand for a traded stock forces the price upward. If a stock price starts to rise rapidly, the trend may continue to escalate because the short sellers will likely want out. For example, say a stock rises 15% in one day, those with short positions may be forced to liquidate and cover their position by purchasing the stock. If enough short sellers buy back the stock, the price is pushed even higher.

☑ **Single stock derivatives**

A single transaction equivalent to the simultaneous sale of a put and purchase of a call for a given stock. Single stock futures essentially allow investors to sell a stock short without waiting for a downtick as would otherwise be required.

☑ **Sleeping Beauty (U.S.)**

A desirable company, often with considerable cash on its balance sheet, that is vulnerable to a takeover attempt by another company.

☑ **Small firm effect**

The tendency of small firms (in terms of total market capitalization) to outperform the stock market (consisting of both large and small firms).

☑ **Special Delivery**

Delivery and payment beyond fourteen days' limit subject to the exact date being specified at the time of contract and authorised by the Stock Exchange.

☑ **Specified Shares**

A group of equity shares in which carry forward of transactions from one settlement period to the next is permitted.

☑ **Spin off**

When a company decides that a subsidiary needs to stand on its own, it might do a spin-off, distributing shares of the new entity to existing shareholders, or selling the new business to its managers or even its employees.

☑ **Split**

Sub-division of a share of large denomination into shares of smaller denominations. Also means subdivision of holdings.

☑ **Spoofing**

Placing a limit order at a better price than the current market price for purchase or sale of thinly traded scrips and then endeavouring to cancel the initial limit order in order to induce buy or sell.

☑ **Spot Delivery Contract**

A contract which provides for

1. Actual delivery of securities and the payment of a price therefore either on the same day as the date of the contract or on the next day, the actual period taken for the despatch of the securities or the remittance of money therefore through the post being excluded from the computation of the period aforesaid if the parties to the contract do not reside in the same town or locality;
2. Transfer of the securities by the depository from the account of a beneficial owner to the account of another beneficial owner when such securities are dealt with by a depository.

☑ **Stag**
1. An applicant, for a new issue of shares, who hopes to sell the shares on allotment at a profit once trading commences in the secondary market.
2. A speculator who buys and sells stocks rapidly for fast profits.

☑ **Stagflation**

The combination of sluggish economic growth, high unemployment and high inflation.

☑ **Stagnation**

Period of low volume and inactive trading on the securities market.

☑ **Staggered Board (U.S.)**

A board of directors in which only a certain number of the directors say, a third, are elected each year. This is considered one effective method through which a company might protect itself against an unwelcome takeover attempt. With a staggered board, an outside group could only obtain control of a minority of the board of directors in any given year, since holdover directors elected in earlier years would continue to serve.

☑ **Stakeholder**

Any individual or group who has an interest in a firm; in addition to shareholders and bondholders, includes labor, consumers, suppliers, the local community and so on.

☑ **Stamp Duty**

The ad valorem duty payable by buyer for transfer of shares in his name. Also payable on contracts issued by a stock-broker.

☑ **Standard Price**

The standard price of a security is generally worked out as a weighted average price of all recorded transactions for that security adjusted to the nearest rupee.

☑ **Stock dividend**

A dividend paid to stockholders in shares of stock of the issuing corporation, issued to stockholders or record out of the unissued stock of the corporation, involving no payment of cash, and used to reflect positive interest in the security.

☑ **Stock Index Future**

A futures contract whose price varies in line with the movements of a stock market index.

☑ **Stock lending**

The lending of a security by the registered owner, to an authorized third party, for a fixed or open period of time, for an agreed consideration secured by collateral. The demand to borrow securities comes mainly from market makers to cover short positions or take arbitrage opportunities.

☑ **Stop Loss Order (or) Stop Order**

An order to sell a security when it declines to a specified price.

☑ **Stock exchange**

Any body of individuals, whether incorporated or not, constituted for the purpose of assisting, regulating or controlling the business of buying, selling or dealing in securities.

☑ **Stock option**

The right to purchase shares of common stock in accordance with an agreement, upon payment of a specified amount; a compensation scheme under which executives are granted options to purchase common stock over an extended option period at a stated price.

☑ Stock splits

A distribution of company's own capital stock to existing stockholders with the purpose of reducing the market price of the stock, which would hopefully increase the demand for the shares.

☑ Straddle

A combination strategy in which the same position is taken in the same number of puts as calls.

☑ Straight through processing (STP)

The processing of a trade, whose data is compliant with internal and external requirements, through systems from post-execution through settlement without manual intervention.Simply put it means seamless integration of trades from initiation to settlement without manual intervention.

☑ Strike Price

The price, in contracts for put options and call options, at which the option can be exercised. Sometimes called the exercise price or basis price.

☑ Subaccount

Sub-account includes foreign corporates or foreign individuals and those institutions, established or incorporated outside India and those funds, or portfolios, established outside India, whether incorporated or not, on whose behalf investments are proposed to be made in India by a Foreign Institutional Investor.

☑ **Sub broker**

Any person not being a member of a stock exchange who acts on behalf of a stock-broker as an agent or otherwise for assisting the investors in buying, selling or dealing in securities through such stock-brokers.

☑ **Subscribed Capital**

The amount of equity and preference capital subscribed to by the shareholders either fully or partly paid up with calls in arrears.

☑ **Swap**

A financial transaction which exploits arbitrage opportunities between markets and in which two counter parties agree to exchange streams of payments over time according to a predetermined rule.

☑ **Swap buyback**

The sale of an interest rate swap by one counterparty to the other, effectively ending the swap.

☑ **Swap reversal**

An Interest rate swap designed to end counterparty's role in another Interest rate swap, accomplished by counterbalancing the original swap in maturity, reference rate, and notional amount.

☑ **Swaption**

Options on interest rate swaps. The buyer of a swaption has the right to enter into an interest rate swap agreement by some specified date in the future. The swaption agreement will specify whether the buyer of the swaption will be a fixed-rate receiver or a fixed-rate payer. The writer of the swaption becomes the counterparty to the swap if the buyer exercises.

☑ **Sweat equity**

A sweat equity share is an equity share issued by the company to employees or directors at a discount or for consideration other than cash for providing know-how or making available rights in the nature of intellectual property rights or value additions.

☑ **Society for Worldwide Interbank Financial Telecommunications (SWIFT)**

A dedicated computer network to support funds Transfers messages internationally between over 900 member banks world-wide.

☑ **Switching**

When a trust manager group has a stable of investments, it sometimes allows investors to switch between them. It may or may not charge a fee for this right or grant a discount to existing investors.

☑ **Synchronized or Pre-arranged trading**

Trading on the electronic screen in such a way that trades are put simultaneously in the system of the stock exchange with prior understanding with counterparty by synchronizing the logging in or of trades so that desired quantity matches at desired price.

☑ **Systemic risk**

Risk that affects an entire financial market or system, and not just specific participants. It is not possible to avoid systemic risk through diversification.

☑ **Takeover panel**

An acquirer who proposes to acquire shares through a mode which is not specifically covered under takeover regulations may seek exemption from the applicability of the provisions of the offer process by making an application. SEBI has constituted a panel consisting of independent persons to examine such applications which is called the Takeover Panel.

☑ **Taligating**

When a broker or advisor purchases or sells a security for their client(s) and then immediately does the same transaction in his/her own account.This is not illegal like front running, but is still considered to be unethical because the broker is usually placing a trade for his/her own account based on what the client knows (like inside information).

☑ **Target Company**

A Target company is a listed company i.e. whose shares are listed on any stock exchange and whose shares or voting rights are acquired/ being acquired or whose control is taken over/being taken over by an acquirer.

☑ **Technical Position**

Condition of the market created by various internal factors and opposed to external forces.

☑ **Tender Offer**

Tender offer means an offer by a company to buy back its specified securities through a letter of offer from the holders of the specified securities of the company.

☑ **Thin markets**

Characterized by relatively few transactions per unit of time and where price fluctuations are high relative to the volume of trade.

☑ **Tombstone**

An advertisement placed in financial newspaper or magazine to announce the completion of a syndicated loan or a new issue of securities. It is called a tombstone because it consists of little more than a list of names and dates. The names are those of borrower (who pays for tombstone) and of the financial institutions which participated in the deal. They are ordered in strict seniority , the size of the typeface indicating their importance in the deal. Within the same rank, participants are listed strictly alphabetically. The more the tombstones there are, the less dead is the market.

☑ **Tracking error**

When using an indexing or any other benchmarking strategy, the amount by which the performance of the portfolio differed from that of the benchmark.

☑ **Tracking Stock**

A class of company share designed to "track" the performance of a particular division or subsidiary of a company, also sometimes known as a letter stock or targeted stock. A tracking stock is usually issued by a large (old) conglomerate when it feels that the value of a small (young) offspring is not being fully appreciated by the market.

☑ **Trade netting**

A legally enforceable consolidation and offsetting of individual trades into net amounts of securities and money due between trading partners or among members of a clearing system. A netting of trades which is not legally enforceable is position netting.

☑ **Trading member**

A member of the derivatives exchange or derivatives segment of a stock exchange who settles the trade in the clearing corporation or clearing house through a clearing member.

☑ **Trading Volume**

Trading volume means the number of shares that are traded on a particular day.

☑ **Transaction statement**

The depository participant gives a Transaction Statement periodically, which will detail current balances and various transactions made through the depository account. If so desired, DP may provide the Transaction Statement at intervals shorter than the stipulated ones, probably at a cost.

☑ **Transfer Agents**

An agent designated by the company to carry out the function of transfer of shares.

☑ **Transfer Forms**

Forms which have to accompany the share certificate for effecting a valid transfer of ownership form the seller to the buyer.

☑ **Transfer Stamps**

Under provisions of the Indian Stamp Act, the transfer deed for the transfer of shares is required to be stamped at the rate of 0.50 per Rs 100/- or part there of, calculated on the amount of consideration.

☑ **Transferee**

The buyer of the securities in whose favour the securities are bought to be registered is known as the Transferee.

☑ **Transferor**

The seller of the security is the transferor of the security.

☑ **Treasury Bills**

A short term bearer discount security issued by governments as a means of financing their cash requirements. Treasury Bills play an important role in the local money market because most banks are required to hold them as part of their reserve requirements and because central bank open market operations undertaken in the process of implementing monetary policy are usually conducted in the treasury bill market.

☑ **Trust Deed**

Detailed legal document which sets out in precise legal terms the rules under which a trust works, its aim, the fees and charges that are created, plus the responsibilities of the Manager and the Trustee. As per SEBI Debenture Trustee rules, trust deed is a deed executed by the body corporate in favour of the trustees named therein for the benefit of the debenture holders.

☑ **Trust Promoter**

Person or company responsible for attracting investors into a unit trust or mutual fund.

☑ **Trustee**

Legal custodian who looks after all the monies invested in a unit trust or mutual fund.

☑ **Two Sided Market (U.S.)**

The obligation imposed on market makers that they make both firm bids and firm offers in each security in which they deal.

☑ **Underlying**

The designated financial instrument which must be delivered in completion of an option or futures contract.

☑ **Underwriter**

One who does underwriting. A financial organization that handles sales of new securities which a company or municipality wishes to sell in order to raise money. Typically the underwriters will guarantee subscription to securities say, an issue of equity from the company at a stated price, and are under an obligation to purchase securities upto the amount they have underwritten, should the public not subscribe for the issue.

☑ **Underwriting**

An agreement with or without conditions to subscribe to the securities of a body corporate when the existing shareholders of such body corporate or the public do not subscribe to the securities offered to them.

☑ **Unit Holders**

Investors in unit trusts / mutual funds.

☑ **Unit of trading**

The minimum number of shares of a company which are accepted for normal trading on the stock exchange. All transactions are generally done in multiple of trading units. Odd lots are generally traded at a small discount.

☑ Unmatched Transactions

A check is carried out to find out whether the purchases and sales as reported by the members match. A list of those transactions which do not match are called unmatched transactions.

☑ Unsystematic Risk

Also called the diversifiable risk, residual risk, or company-specific risk, the risk that is unique to a company such as a strike, the outcome of unfavourable litigation, or a natural catastrophe.

☑ Upstairs market

A network of trading desks for the major brokerage firms and institutional investors that communicate with each other by means of electronic display systems and telephones to facilitate block trades and program traders.

☑ Value investing

The investment style of attempting to buy underpriced stocks that have the potential to perform well and appreciate in terms of price.

☑ Value at Risk (VAR)

VAR is the maximum loss over a target horizon such that there is a low, prespecified probability that the actual loss will be larger.

☑ **Vanilla Issue**

A straight fixed rate issue which has terms and conditions usually accepted as being conventional to a particular securities market.

☑ **Vanishing companies**

Companies which have not complied with specific provisions of the listing agreement and regulations of the stock exchanges, and are not physically traceable at the registered address mentioned in the offer document.

☑ **Venture Capital**

Professional moneys co-invested with the entrepreneur usually to fund an early stage, more risky venture. Offsetting the high risk is the promise of higher return that the investor takes. A venture capitalist not only brings in moneys as "equity capital" (i.e. without security/charge on assets) but also brings on to the table extremely valuable domain knowledge ,business contacts, brand equity, strategic advice, etc. He is a fixed interval investor, whom the entrepreneurs approach without the risk of "takeover".

☑ **Venture Capital Fund**

A fund established in the form of a trust or a company including a body corporate and registered under the SEBI venture capital fund regulations which - has a dedicated pool of capital, raised in a manner specified in the regulations and invests in venture capital undertaking in accordance with the regulations.

☑ **Venture Capital Undertaking**

A domestic company whose shares are not listed an a recognised stock exchange in India and which is engaged in the business for providing services, production or manufacture of article or things or does not include such activities or sectors which are specified in the negative list by the Board with the approval of the Central Government.

☑ **Vertical spread**

Buying and selling puts or calls of the same expiration month but with different strike prices.

☑ **Vesting**

The process by which the employee is given the right to apply for shares of the company against the option granted to him in pursuance of Employee Stock Option Scheme.

☑ **Volatility**

Volatility equates to the variability of returns from an investment. It is an acceptable substitute for risk; the greater the volatility, the greater is the risk that an investment will not turn out as hoped because its market price happens to be on the downswing of a bounce at the time that it needs to be cashed in. The problem is that future volatility is hard to predict and measures of past volatility can, themselves, be variable, depending on how frequently returns are measured (weekly or monthly, for example) and for how long. Therefore, putting expectations of future volatility into predictive models is of limited use, but resorting to using past levels of volatility is equally limited.

☑ Volume of Trading

The total number of shares which changes hands in a particular company's securities. This information is useful in explaining and interpreting fluctuation in share prices.

☑ Voluntary delisting

Delisting of securities of a body corporate voluntarily by a promoter or an acquirer or any other person other than the stock exchange

☑ Voting Rights

The entitlement of a shareholder to exercise vote in the general meeting of a company

☑ Warrant

An options contract often sold with another security. For instance, corporate bonds may be sold with warrants to buy common stock of that corporation. Warrants are generally detachable.

☑ Wash sales

A wash sale involves a person, either directly or indirectly, being both the buyer and seller of securities in the same transaction, so that there is no actual change in ownership of the securities. The manipulator will undertake frequent trades hoping to attract other investors who note the increased turn over in the security. The manipulator aims to gain financially through creating a small price differential between the buy and sell rates of the security in question.

☑ White Knight (U.S.)

A friendly bidder, willing to offer more for a target share than an existing hostile bidder to rescue a company that is about to fall into the hands of an unwelcome suitor. They are usually persuaded by the company that is subject to a hostile bid to come to its rescue.

☑ Window Dressing

A manoeuvre often engaged in by companies, banks, mutual funds etc., at the end of the accounting period in order to impress stock holders who will be receiving the report showing that funds are better managed and invested than what might have been drawn up.

☑ Winner's Curse

The tendency that in a bidding contest or in some types of auctions, the winner is the bidder with the highest (over-optimistic) estimate of value. This explains the high frequency of negative returns to acquiring firms in takeovers with multiple bidders.

☑ **Wolf**

Speculators who make a kill in the market.

☑ **Worst case scenario loss**

The worst case loss of a portfolio would be calculated by valuing the portfolio under several scenarios of changes in the underlying prices and volatility. The maximum loss in any situation is referred to as the Worst Scenario Loss.

☑ **Writer**

A person who issues an option. The individual who at the end of the day has to buy or sell the asset on which the option is written, should the person who holds the option wish to exercise his rights.

☑ **X Dividend**

A term meaning 'without dividend'. A stock bought on or after the X- dividend day will not pay the purchaser the dividend already declared.

☑ **Yankee Bond (U.S.)**

A bond offering in the U.S. domestic market by a non-U.S. entity registered with the SEC.

☑ **Yield to maturity (YTM)**

The rate of return anticipated on a bond if it is held until the maturity date. YTM is considered a long term bond yield expressed as an annual rate.

☑ **Yuppie Scam (U.S.)**

The name given to Wall Street insider trading scandal after a host of smart young lawyers, bankers and arbitrageurs were found to be in the dealing ring.

☑ **Zero Coupon Bond**

A bond that pays no interest while the investor holds it. It is sold originally at a substantial discount from its eventual maturity value, paying the investor its full face value when it comes due, with the difference between what he paid initially and what he finally collected representing the interest he would have received over the years it was held.

☑ **Zero coupon yield curve**

A yield curve of zero coupon bonds. Market practice is often to derive this curve theoretically from the par yield curve. Frequently used to derive discount factors. Also known as spot yield curve.

www.ingramcontent.com/pod-product-compliance
Lightning Source LLC
Chambersburg PA
CBHW072333150726
47998CB00017B/521